THE BOUNCER

To my mum and my dad. Thank you for showing
me that one way or another, there is a good
story in everything – and this one was worth
persisting with.

'... this seemed strange to me but not strange if you know what I mean.
Kids just are wherever they are and do whatever they're doing, you
know. This is where I was and this is what I was doing.'
Josh 'J' Cody, from the movie *Animal Kingdom*, 2010, writer David
Michod

THE BOUNCER

HEATH LANDER

FINCH PUBLISHING

SYDNEY

The Bouncer

First published in 2013 in Australia and New Zealand by Finch Publishing Pty Limited, ABN 49 057 285 248, Suite 2207, 4 Daydream Street, Warriewood, NSW, 2102, Australia.

13   8 7 6 5 4 3 2 1

National Library of Australia Cataloguing-in-Publication entry:
Lander, Heath, author.

The bouncer / Heath Lander.
9780987419651 (paperback)
Bouncers--Victoria--Melbourne--Biography. Bars (Drinking establishments)--Victoria--Melbourne--Biography. Bars (Drinking establishments)--Victoria--Melbourne--Anecdotes.

363.289092

Edited by Emend Editing
Editorial assistance by Megan Drinan
Text typeset in Adobe Garamond by Pier Vido
Cover design by Ingrid Kwong
Printed by McPhersons Printing

Contents

Chapter 1
SPECIAL GUEST

'YOU GOTTA GO, MATE.'

'What?'

'You're out.'

'Fuck off. You can't throw me out.'

'Pig's arse. You can walk out now or so help me I'll punch your lights out and drag you out by the hair.'

'You'll lose your job ya dumb cunt.'

'I don't give a rat's arse. Be worth this fuckin' job for the chance to change the way you look.'

'Where's the manager? Let me talk to him.'

'Fuck that. Start walking.'

He walked in front of me through the carpeted corridor and into the chill-out area. Down the corridor towards the stairs, the street four flights down. He turned around.

'Come on then cunt. You're going to have to hit me to make ...'

I punched him hard straight in the face. His head rocked back and he stared at me.

'Keep walking.'

'What the fuck, what the fuck, what the fuck ...'

'Actually,' I said. 'Why don't you stay?' I pulled him back into the club by his shirt front and started punching him as hard as I could, as fast as I could, in the face and chest, my knee pinning him down. Over and over, grunting and swearing as I worked until hands lifted me off.

Chapter 2
ANCESTORS

THERE WAS LITTLE IN MY EARLY YEARS TO SUGGEST I WOULD WORK IN nightclub security. I grew up in a green, middle-class Melbourne suburb. The house was scattered with photos of a plump Indian guru and my parents meditated morning and evening. Mum was a drama teacher at a girls' college and Dad was a drama lecturer. She dragged him out of England by his pubic hair to Canada where they lived on a bus with the other members of their travelling theatre. I was born in the frozen foothills of the Rocky Mountains and, before my first birthday, came to Australia when my father took a position at Melbourne University.

My parents wore kaftans. Mum had a heavy brass ankh that my sister and I used for dress-ups when we needed a witch doctor. We spent summers camping on a nudist beach with other naked folk. Guitar and bongo jams by the fire, kids making up plays for the parents to watch. A whole lot of natural fibre, good vibes and perhaps free love. I was too young to know. But they weren't hippies. They would be pained to admit it but there remained too much latent English properness about them for true hippiedom. It's in the photos from the time. A little too much posture, not enough politics. Until my mum came out of her closet aged 40 or so, they made a safe, supportive, loving and extremely un-violent home for my sister and I.

They were bored by drug use. They were into drama, but not performance art or happenings. My father staged Shakespeare, Brecht and Chekhov. They were intelligent people inspired by the zeitgeist.

My childhood diet rarely strayed from vegetables, tofu, brown rice, soggy homemade bread and lentils. Mum's only alternative diet success was her muesli. Oats, nuts, wheatgerm, bran, dried fruits, soaked currants, shredded coconut, lecithin, sesame and sunflower seeds and about ten litres of fresh, real honey. She would bake trays of the stuff. The smell of this baking would travel up out of the urban valley we lived in, like the ring of a town bell. Whether I was stealing pigeons from the old man at the top of the hill, finger-painting with my sister or sewing a new sleeping bag for my Barbie and Snoopy dolls, the smell of a muesli batch called me.

My sister and I would make guerrilla attacks on the kitchen, escaping with piping hot clumps of sticky, fresh muesli scalding our palms. The grains were soft with honey and fell apart deliciously in our mouths.

The education my parents chose for me pointed further again from a career in nightclub security. I went to a tiny alternative school. The grounds were vast and unkempt, with weeds as tall as teachers. Massive oak and eucalypt trees to climb. No uniform except mud. We called our teachers by their first name and had weekly school meetings where our matriarch principal, with her bizarre whippet-labrador cross, would preside. The physical-education program was traditional Israeli dancing on Tuesday mornings. If I wanted a lie-down during story time that was fine, even in grade six.

The school was more interested in instilling community values than a competitive edge. To fill this void, Dad sent me to the local judo club. Two o'clock every Saturday afternoon in a scout hall. It was an ageing firetrap of a building. Peeling weatherboards and a gravel car park riddled with weeds. The teacher was a huge man. Towering over me, as wide as an old growth trunk, he had a flaming red beard and hair, small steel-rimmed spectacles and in his weathered, greyish judo uniform, frayed black belt and bare feet, he was terrifying to me. He instructed me to bow at the door.

'Bow?'

'Bend at the hips.'

'What for?'

'The ancestors.'

The ancestors could have been a music group.

I loved what we did in the class. Learning to throw people with our legs, our hips or over our shoulders, and how to control an opponent once you had thrown them. It never felt like fighting, though. The soft cotton weave of my uniform – gi (pronounced ghee) – was more like pyjamas than battle cladding, the grappling more like play than combat.

After three years of classes, when I was thirteen, my teacher entered me in a state competition. I was accustomed to winning in the safety of the club and thrashing my sister. I'd never competed against people I didn't know and trust. I thought a state judo tournament would be lots of kids like me with love and mung beans in their veins getting together to have a bit of a cuddle.

My first and only fight didn't last long. I stepped onto the mat, bowed to the big Greek boy opposite me …

'HAJIME', the referee called.

My opponent charged at me, turning like mercury into a hip throw and before I could even exhale, he had me on the ground and was bearing down, squeezing the life out of me. All I remember is trying not to cry or piss myself. On the way home I cried so hard and long into Mum's lap she may as well have pissed herself.

I didn't stop doing judo immediately, but the fun was gone. I felt I had fallen short of my teacher's expectations. It wasn't just a desire for his approval or a need to be at the top of the class. I wanted to honour what he had taught. All that stuff about respect for the ancestors. To do judo until you were eighty, you would have to get beaten a lot. Those old buggers must have been resilient as hell. More resilient than this little thirteen-year-old.

Chapter 3
FROM BAHAI TO BRUNSWICK STREET

WHILE I WAS AT UNIVERSITY STUDYING SCULPTURE AND EDUCATION, I TOOK A break from drinking alcohol and gave up smoking. As a substitute I decided to take on some physical training. Someone suggested a martial art called Capoeira.

Capoeira was beautiful, fluid and graceful. The people in the class were young and confident. To watch Capoeira being performed was seductive, its daring and agility rewarded with cheers. I was excited by stories that once upon a time on the docks of Bahia, Capoeiristas had transformed their acrobatics into battle moves by strapping blades to their whirling, tumbling toes. But this was nothing to do with my main interest. Capoeira was made for virile youth. There were lots of women in the group, the guys looked great from their training, and I was as horny as a sackful of jack rabbits.

On a hot summer's night in Collingwood, a block west of Hoddle Street in a pocket of streets that take their name from regional centres, some friends and I made our way to a party. I had been to Capoeira class that afternoon and was cartwheeling and spinning around the group as the sun set. Brunswick Street lay ten blocks ahead of us and the party was somewhere in between. We were recently enough out of high school to still be a large social cluster but long enough to have grown apart a little.

'What's this Cap-a-air-a stuff you're doing these days?' Rob asked me.

'It's a Brazilian martial art that was developed by slaves. They disguised the movements within dance and music so that their keepers wouldn't know they were training to fight.' I spilled out the treadmill of rhetoric we picked up from the teacher between cartwheels.

'So it's about fighting then?' Rob said. When he was sober he was a very gentle, quiet guy. Drunk, he was antagonistic and prone to inciting fights.

'Yeah, for sure,' I replied.

'So all this cartwheeling and twisting around on all fours, you can use that to fight then?'

'Yeah.'

'What if I do this?'

Right in the middle of a cartwheel he hip and shouldered me. Because I was upside down his hip hit my face and his shoulder hit my crutch. I was knocked away from him and forced to roll uncomfortably onto my shoulder against the asphalt. In the time it took for me to fall down, stand up and brush myself down, my love of Capoeira evaporated.

I mistook physical fitness and dexterity for fighting nous. Because I had learnt to move my legs quickly through the motion of a kick, I had slipped into thinking that I was a proficient kicker. The movements in Capoeira are potentially effective for fighting, devastating even. Learning to use them that way, however, would require much more time and a different way of training.

I went back to Capoeira classes but where before I'd seen grace, speed and beauty, now I saw vulnerability, showiness and pretence. I drifted away, back into the morass of the inactive. I was afraid of a tiny voice within whispering that I was weak. I remembered the claustrophobia of being pinned down in that one and only judo tournament and crying in the back seat of the car. I heard myself thinking that I was spineless and timid.

I ran into an old girlfriend in Smith Street one day. It was afternoon, late in the summer and the pavement throbbed with months' worth of heat. In the shadow of the twenty-four hour supermarket I chatted with Rachel.

'How's Capoeira?'

'I stopped.'

'How come? You were so bloody nuts about it. Last time I saw you it was all you could talk about.'

'I know. Moved on I guess.'

'Bullshit, you don't just move on. What happened?'

'You could say I got into a fight.'

'What! You're shittin' me!'

Rachel was a short, beautiful girl who had fallen for me in between overseas travel. She always said she wished that I had gone travelling with her, but that she knew I was too much of a mumma's boy to do it. She knew me pretty well.

'Not really a fight, someone just sort of tested me, and the Capoeira let me down.'

'But you've only been doing it six months, you've hardly given it a chance.'

She was right. No one could expect to be a lean mean street fighting machine after six months' training three times a week. I was being harsh on myself and Capoeira. The problem was that even after training for six months, I had no idea what to do when Rob charged me. I had been confused, surprised and upside down.

'Yeah, yeah, what are you, my mother? Look I just sort of had a realisation about it, I was getting a bit carried away, thinking it was something more than it was.'

'You hardly gave it time to be more than a hobby.'

'Whatever.'

It was a weak answer and Rachel was not kind enough to let it go. 'You're just too much of a dreamer. I saw it in your eyes last time we talked. You had some fantasy going that you were this bad-arse Brazilian street fighter. Now someone's come along and challenged that and you can't face it.'

'Jesus Christ, Rach. Aren't we supposed to be just catching up with each other? It's the middle of Smith Street. When I need analysis, I'll call a counsellor.'

'That's it with you isn't it? You're always ready with the character breakdowns and trauma assessments for other people, but when the heat's on, you start deflecting.'

I was starting to feel a little hunted and she was looking dangerous.

'What was it about that stuff that got you fired up? Was it putting you in touch with the warrior within?'

'Oh, come on, we're not even going out anymore.'

'Well? Was it? Was it you getting in touch with your masculinity? There's nothing wrong with it. In fact, it's probably about fucking time.'

'Well, if we really are going there, I suppose it was that. I started feeling physically strong, and emotionally as well.'

'And you got a reality check and felt silly for falling for your own fantasy?'

'You seem to know me pretty well.'

'Shut up. It's exactly what you did to me, you were always talking up the idea of us travelling together until I put the hard word on to actually do it and you went all fuckin' flaccid on me.'

'Is that what this is about? Us?'

'No, dickhead. Us ended when I left you and went across South America. This is about you. You live in your head. Your reality is defined by daydreams. There's nothing wrong with being masculine. You could have, or should have, just told me that all you wanted was a fuck before I headed off again. I would have respected that but you dragged it out. There's nothing wrong with being strong, you need it, but for fuck's sake, if you're going to crawl back into your bloody head after the first time you get a shock, fuck, I mean, don't you see the futility of that?'

'Yes. Thank you very much, I do.'

'Well why don't you bloody well keep going? One of the bouncers at the Royal, Alby, runs a kung fu club. He's a great guy. You could try training with him. He definitely knows how to fight. I've seen him.'

I was feeling pretty wounded, but what she was saying was true.

'I gotta go, it's nice seeing you Heath, I love you but you gotta grow up, get a grip on the real world. See ya.'

She kissed me and walked away.

Chapter 4

A TASTE FOR THE FIGHT

THE KUNG FU CLUB WAS ON THE FIRST FLOOR OF A BUILDING IN THE CBD. THE building had low ceilings, cork floor and banks of fluorescent lights. Just inside the door was a boxing ring. I'd never seen one before. Large punching bags hung along the walls looking swollen and tired. Across the ring was an office stuffed with merchandise. Beyond the office was a rough and well-used collection of weights and barbells. Behind them were two rooms partitioned by folding walls, floored with big, square, interlocking foam mats. In the far one a karate class was in session. The teacher stood facing the class in a frayed suit stained fawn by years of sweat. A peeling black belt held his lapels together. The students in their white uniforms moved rigidly through strict movements.

I went to the desk. A young bald man with a long nose and aggressive eyes sat flicking through a martial arts magazine. He was wearing his karate uniform – a gi, I remembered it was called – and a green belt. I had no idea what the belt's colour symbolised but by his manner I was ready to believe he was a killer.

'I'm here for a kung fu class. Am I in the right place?'

His eyes were cold as he said, 'This is a karate school, but there is a kung fu class that starts in fifteen minutes. First class is free.'

He looked back to his magazine. I could have felt more welcomed.

'Thanks.' He directed me to the second of the rooms. The mats on the floor were green. The roof was low and hanging on the walls were swords, rubber knives, and in one corner there was a collection of eight-foot lengths of dowel. I was alone, the only noise was the loud counting in Japanese from the adjacent room and the shhh of the karateka's feet moving over the mat.

I had come partly because the teacher was an artist. I imagined he must have a sensitive side as well as physical prowess. However, Rachel's comments were the real reason I was here. My reluctance to step into the stream of the real, concrete world had cost me a sexy journey through South America and a relationship.

A man entered the room. He was shorter than me. Barrel chested, with skin as pale and soft as a child's. His legs were short and solid.

'Here for kung fu?' he asked. I shook his hand which, in contrast to his face, was calloused and leathery. He was older than I had expected but his eyes were wet slate grey and piercing.

'Yeah. Hi. Are you Alby?'

'Yep.'

That was it for pleasantries. A rough warm-up and we started to punch hand-held bags. Alby gave me technique tips as we went and though I felt adrift and inadequate, it was exhilarating to be hitting something. With every novice thud of fist against polyester I felt a little more connected to the real world that Rachel said was lost to me.

Alby had a gruff, unavailable way of teaching. He did the action as he wanted it done and your job was to copy it. He didn't suffer questions well and preferred to increase the work rather than stop and clarify technique. It was early March when I started. The only other students were a myopic woman, who was clearly better suited to yoga, and Crazy Chris. Alby called him this openly. Chris didn't mind. He *was* crazy. He couldn't generally remember his right from his left and anything past the most basic punches was beyond him. It didn't stop him talking constantly about how he was going to join the Turkish army. It didn't stop him hitting anything he could as hard as he could whenever he could, either.

Chris was at least six foot four with a considerable hunch. Three months after I first arrived at the class, Alby took us all out of our little room to the boxing ring. We put on bulbous full-size gloves and Alby told me to hop in the ring with Chris. There were other students by now and I would have preferred to be against any one of them for my first-ever sparring round.

My knees would have shaken no less had I been climbing into the centre of Madison Square Garden. Chris was amped. He bashed his gloves together like a pro and stared me down. I stared at my toes and tried to think through a growing wall of panic.

'Right. Light punches you two, just move around. Get a feel for the ring. Off you go.'

Chris charged at me and threw a huge punch. He knocked me off my feet. My nose stung and my eyes were watering. Chris stood over me, breathing hard.

'Chris, Jesus, take it easy,' Alby reprimanded. He turned to me.

'You right? Want to stop?' I didn't say yes. I stood up wiped my eyes and checked my legs were working.

'Right. Now TAKE IT EASY. Off you go.'

Chris stepped in and swung another huge punch at me. This time I got out of the way. The weight he had in the punch had carried his right arm and shoulder a long way to his left. There was no thought in my action. I guess it was the adrenalin from just having been knocked on my arse. I unloaded everything I had – not much as I was a novice, sixty-five-kilo white boy – into a punch that more out of luck than dexterity landed on Chris's jaw. He looked shocked for a moment then he had a turn on his arse.

Chris got angry and stormed out of the class and into the street in shorts, a singlet and big, fat, red boxing gloves. He didn't come back for months.

Alby didn't reprimand me at all. None of us knew quite what to make of it. Some other students had turns in the ring and I watched, but I didn't see much. I was frozen in that moment when I saw the vulnerability of my opponent. I had plugged myself into the same impulse that throws the spear and pulls the trigger. I was drunk on my own testosterone.

Alby ran two classes during the week and one on Saturday. I attended all of them. It wasn't long before I was meeting him on Wednesday mornings to join him on his training session.

When he told me he had a job lined up for me at the Royal, I assumed it was as a barman. Not as a bouncer. I'd given up a place in a masters degree and a teaching position because I wanted to spend a few years working out the direction I wanted to take with my sculpture.

Since I had begun training with Alby I had barely set foot in my studio. Most of the time that I would once have spent making sculptures, I now spent watching kung fu movies.

Chapter 5
THE ROYAL

I knew the Royal well from the outside. Rachel worked there when we were going out together. On that first day I wore four or five shirts to try and make myself look bulkier.

The first thing I remember clearly was Alby, in the middle of the room, moving with calm authority while the crowd parted before him. In all the noise and madness, this man was a still point. Clint Eastwood in the Wild West. Keanu in *The Matrix.*

Everything else I remember from that night was just atmosphere, the backdrop to that big bear of a man ambling at me through the crowd. Whatever else kept me from leaving the job in years to come – money, laziness, habit – it was this moment that drew me to it. This moment when, for an instant, I knew what I wanted to be.

I wasn't born to the role. I had to learn it. Natural bouncers don't have epiphanies that transform them and make them want to be a bouncer. They just find themselves there and accept it.

Alby had decided I was ready to work with him. I was terrified but not prepared to risk disappointing him by turning it down. From a man who rarely praised, I took it as the platform for my next stage of training. If Alby had used gradings in his club, the story might have been quite different.

The Royal was in a busy strip of bars and pubs. In my childhood I had come to the area and eaten with my father when it was predominantly lined with butchers, bakers, laundromats, delis and milk bars.

When I was a kid, the Royal was where you went to find trouble. It was full of men who came and went without having a drink, rarely sitting down. There were gang members, drug dealers and standover men with bad hair, speed habits and broken families, cheap tracksuits and short fuses. Old men with bruisy tattoos and no teeth sat at the stools muttering.

When I started at the Royal, the street was still dangerous enough to be appealing to outsiders, but safe enough for artists and students from the nearby university to live in. Bob was the new owner's name. He had added the smell of lattes and macchiatos to the smell of wine and smoke and dried piss transforming the pub into a nouveau riche oasis, offering the moneyed middle a stop on the way home to the eastern suburbs. The place printed money.

The main bar had two managers. Billy, a big balding man who struggled with small talk. He barked instructions or whispered conspiratorily about his masturbation habits. The other manager was Mark. Shorter, darker and mysterious, he had a soft voice and a gentle handshake. He exuded authority. He was balding too, but where Billy looked damaged by his hair loss, Mark wore it shorn close and retained a certain elegance. Mark defied the sweat and smell, and the late, long hours of the job. Hours in the gym and solarium kept him looking youthful and strong. He was the go-to guy for problems. He was never late, never missed a shift, always ordered things on time and remembered names. He never gave away free drinks but still made people feel special.

Heterosexual, post-adolescent and earnest. Three things the bar staff all had in common. Students, travellers, actors, artists, musicians, all on their way somewhere or paying something off. They bounced off each other behind the bar and fucked each other between shifts. The politics of the bar staff played out each night like a bad soap. He fucked her and she blew him. She's pissed off with her and they don't talk to people anymore now that they are in love. Arseholes, hate all of you. Wanna drink? They wore uniform black T-shirts. The faces changed regularly but not the proclivities or their intensity.

Homosexual, late-twenties and devoutly cynical. Three things the restaurant staff had in common. They tolerated customers' requests the way mechanics tolerate complaints. They had forgotten more about food and wine than the patrons would ever know. They wore starched white shirts, excellent ties and neat black waistcoats. Some had been at the pub so long and behaved with such rudeness that people believed they owned the place.

These queens saw themselves as hospitality aristocracy. They strode around the restaurant like mating peacocks, handing out judgements on orders, outfits and partners for the night. One, Anthony, otherwise known as Elaine, had told a patron to leave when she complained that the salmon was undercooked, and dragged her out when she refused.

The maitre d' in the restaurant was Imelda. Or Ian. In command of the waiting staff was Mai, a gorgeous, lesbian Chinese dynamo who changed her hair colour every week. Kathy, the only hetero on the floor, was gorgeous, aloof, and in the middle of her zoology masters. Alan/ Mary, tall, spindly and alcoholic, left to sell designer tap fittings and Angie, a floor manager, was forty, four-feet tall and volatile as only a short lesbian can be.

The head chef was of basque parents but looked like a South-American cowboy. Swarthy, gorgeous and outrageously gay, he ran the kitchen as he ran his boyfriend – with love, unrelenting and until the wee hours of the morning.

Most nights, the place burst at the seams. The bar staff raced like caged monkeys, wild with adrenalin, sliding past each other as they mixed silver shakers of cocktails and pulled glass after frothing glass of beer. Busboys with cord-like forearms worked through the crowd with trays of empty glasses balanced above the swaying heads. Women screamed together in glee, free and beckoning. Sweating, uncouth and uncoordinated circles of men swayed in song or discussion or leering admiration of a woman.

The noise was cacophonous – squeals, swearing, singing, the yells of those at the bar who could not get service, trays of glasses thrown into washers, hot water sluicing, the crashing rattle as they were added to teetering stacks of trays, the pop of a champagne cork, giggles, bar staff yelling, the roar of traffic through the open doors and beneath it all the bassey beat of the speakers.

The kitchen was a mad symphony of movement, the staff shaky from three back-to-back shifts and no sleep for two nights propped up by amphetamines and the possibility of sleep tomorrow. A bank of gas burners littered with black, pressed steel pans that at the touch of scarred and scalded hands skipped and danced around each other, their contents flicked and shlooped into fountains and eddies.

At the back of the room, removed from everyone in a crazed and steaming corner, was the dishwasher. A stooped young man with purple hair and pierced ears, he moved with grace and speed. His arms whirled around him like a raging and incarnate shiva.

Chapter 6

BOUNCER SCHOOL

'FIND A SEAT, MATE.'

There were thirty men sitting at tables toying with sandwiches, protein drinks and pens. They were all as big as buses and they were all looking at me. The teacher was broad-shouldered too, in ill-fitting slacks. He wore a button-down polo shirt, his hair carefully parted and his moustache sitting like a small dog across his top lip. His forearms were hairy and hard and his hands were mostly knuckles. I found a seat and wedged myself in. The bus to the left of me spoke.

'G'day mate. George.'

'G'day. Heath. How are ya?'

'Cheers.'

I looked to my right and up. 'Cheers. What's your name?'

'Pieter.'

George the gargantuan Greek and Pieter the Arian hulk. I sat between them like a twig between two wardrobes. As the teacher took focus, I looked around. The pastel walls were dotted with 'recognitions of support' and 'statements of gratitude' in cheap frames. A large gold one held the institute's registration as a government-certified private provider. Another wall, decorated with newspaper clippings, profiled the company's director and the rise of his institution. Older age-stained stories celebrated the achievements of the director as a policeman, while others were public-interest articles about bouncers. A glass cabinet held bouncer accessories: notebooks, pens, T-shirts, caps, batons (retractable and rigid), incident registers, plastic numbers, small metal bars about the length of your fist labelled 'key-chains'.

George was on page eleven and Pieter on page seven. Neither page had anything to do with what the teacher was saying. I flicked through the textbook with its headings on closed-circuit television and laws pertaining to crowd controllers. There were other sections on who was qualified to be employed as a crowd controller, how to respond to a bomb threat and how to initiate evacuation procedures. Liasing with police. Emergency procedures in a multi-storey building. How to respond to a riot situation. None of these things had anything to do with why I thought I was there. If I hadn't been squeezed so tightly between George and Pieter, I might have left then and there.

The class session was a painful stroll through the textbook, punctuated only by stories from the teacher's experience as a policeman. The students loved them. We could have finished our study in two full days but the workload was drawn out over a week. At the end of each day we were given a multiple-choice test. An A4 sheet of twenty questions. If anyone didn't pass they talked about their mistakes with the teacher after class and re-sat the test.

Everyone sat in the same seat as the first morning for the entire week. I hit it off with George and Pieter. They were impressed that I was already working as a bouncer. George brought me scrambled egg and salami sausages. His mum was sending them for me because he had mentioned my size, and she worried I was malnourished. Pieter had been an engineer in Denmark but had moved here to further his body-building training.

Nobody else talked to me all week. Nobody talked to anybody. We were all practising being suspicious of everybody.

'We're not getting taught the right things,' I said to Pieter. 'We aren't being prepared for the job in any practical way. You know, what does a bouncer do? When? How? What are the boundaries? We need better education!'

'No. I think it is fine. I will get my certificate and start to work and learn then,' he said. I turned to George, a bit frustrated.

'This course sucks, eh, George? We're not learning anything.'

'It's OK. I'm going to work for my uncle checking locks in industrial estates. I have to sit through another three weeks of this so I can qualify to carry a gun. It's gonna be grouse.'

People with a security licence might work in a bar like me, but they might also stand guard at a local Safeway for twelve hours, or sit by the door of a jewellery store. They might be in a tiny room watching a bank of closed-circuit television monitors or manning a boom gate at the entrance to somewhere. They might have a gun licence and be driving about in an armoured delivery vehicle. They might be guarding the mosh pit at a rock concert or escorting sportspeople to and from the playing field. All positions requiring skills that were only being touched on in this course.

George and Pieter were confident of their ability to learn and adapt, to respond to situations and learn from them. I was the reluctant one.

I wanted to be cradled, to avoid the truth of the work – that it was varied, unpredictable and, at its core, unteachable.

I took my concerns to the teacher. I explained my sense of not being ready and needing more information. I wanted a referral to other sources, more videos, another course or a book.

'Look, mate, I was a copper for twenty years and I've been working in security and running this place for the last fifteen. No one can teach you to be a bouncer or any other security position that puts you in direct contact with the public. If you're game enough or dumb enough to get into it, then you just have to wait till the shit hits the fan and see what your instincts do. Just 'cos you're small doesn't mean you'll be shit, but it won't help ya. The only way to learn to be a bouncer is to get out there and be one. I'll give ya some advice. Try not to get involved in too much. There's plenty of trouble to go round and it'll find ya soon enough. But if you find it's not for you, don't be too hard on yourself. It's essentially a shit job that people get addicted to. I've always figured it to be the adrenalin.'

On Friday afternoon I walked out into the evening flow of humanity – a qualified crowd controller.

Chapter 7
DICKHEADS AHOY

I REMOVED THE RING FROM MY EYEBROW AND SHAVED MY HEAD. IT WAS A MILD late spring night but I wore five shirts. I sat still all night trying not to sweat or do anything that would betray my true stature. I kept my arms crossed over my chest and when asked questions, grunted as gruffly as I could.

I referred to everyone as mate and avoided eye contact. The laminated number pinned to my chest caught the light in the bar and shone like a night-time sun, heralding the difference between me and everyone else. Except for Alby. Everything I did was a copy of him. The crowd moved around me, pressed up against the wall inside the main door. Grotesque currents of leering faces washed past. A constant din of music, chinking glass and drunken merriment banged against my ears. The shouts of men and women flew about the room disconnected from the tableaux of lechery. Inebriated men would settle briefly around me and ask half-finished, half-heard questions about my night or my life. I tried at first to talk but the noise, their slurring and my anxiety made it futile.

Being on the outside looking into a crowd was completely different to being a part of the throng. For a person in the bar, drinking and carousing, there are focal points – where am I sitting, where are my friends, where is my drink, I need the toilet, I like that girl, that guy has cigarettes, where's my jacket. From the outside, I tried to see everything – who was chatting up who, who went to the toilet and when they came back, who was going to the bar a lot, who was going too much, who was not going at all. My head swam with the stimulus. It was a smudged painting, a fogged photo. Familiar, but without detail. All I really noticed was how much bigger than me everyone else seemed.

I watched Alby. He paid almost no attention to the crowd, staring into the middle distance above their heads. Without warning, when I was looking at the point he seemed fixed on, he was off his stool, moving through the crowd. In two seconds he had gone from sitting glumly on a barstool to halfway through a crowded bar, moving with intent. I followed as best I could, walking into everyone.

By the time I found Alby he was moving back through the crowd towards me. He passed me and was gone. Panting, I found him back on his stool staring over my shoulder.

'What happened?'

'Just had to tell a couple of drunks to leave.'

'Oh. Are they leaving?'

'Yeah, they'll finish their drinks and go.'

Just like that. I wanted to back him up but clearly, he hadn't needed it. I felt like an overdressed decoration.

Three red-faced men came slowly through the crowd like sweaty, toothy ogres. Middle-aged balding men who'd drunk too much after work. I opened the door, which swung inwards, to aid their path. Alby stood by the door, watching them as they approached, one hand scratching his chin and the other resting on his chest. Not tense, but ready. His eyes cool lakes of calm; patient and still. The men approached and I felt sick.

Nodding at both Alby and me, the first man walked out the door. The second man left, laughing and harmless. I began to relax. The third man drew level and stepped past. I sucked in air. The man turned and reached out to pat Alby's shiny head.

'See ya, baldy.'

Alby's hands shot out, slammed into the man's chest. The customer, who weighed at least as much as Alby, was thrown airborne backwards, whump against the door frame, the wind driven out of his lungs. He folded off the wall and out into the street. Alby stepped back, closed the door and sat down.

'Dickheads.'

I leant back against my wall and inhaled again. Awestruck. The economy and precision of Alby's action was the most inspiring lesson he had given me.

I saw my reflection in a window. My collars had been ruffled in the commotion and it was plain to see that I was wearing five layers. Walking to my car that night I saw a gymnasium just down the road from the pub. The next afternoon, shortly after waking, I joined.

Chapter 8

INTO EACH LIFE A LITTLE MASS
MUST FALL

THE GYM WAS A SMALL BUSINESS ON THE THIRD FLOOR OF A RENOVATED warehouse. It had a high steeple ceiling that amplified the weather outside. The walls were pastel tones, purple and soft yellow, and carpet ran from wall to wall. House music oomced out of speakers from dawn till dusk and there was a constant rotation of classes in the big, airy aerobics room. Floor-to-ceiling mirrors were on most walls, and a bank of televisions were suspended in the air above the herd of exercise bikes, step machines and treadmills. Much of the floor space was taken up by cable-type weight machines, with a small free weight section. I was still, according to my programme, only using cable machines.

The gym was owned and run by a man called Bruce. He told everyone that at some stage in his life, perhaps the foetal stage, he too had been small. He was massive. He swaggered around the gym in matching shorts and singlet carrying the equivalent of four or five children in muscle mass. He laboured good naturedly under his burden and couldn't help sneaking furtive, loving glances at his physique whenever he passed a mirror.

The clients of the gym were diverse. The aerobics classes were full of young women and saggy, middle-aged men. On the weights there were inner city twenty-somethings with piercings, tattoos and dreadlocks sweating out toxins from the last dance party; swollen middle-aged professionals staving off decrepitude; healthy, dynamic women that one was well advised not to look at.

There weren't any macho body builders – the colour scheme and soundtrack were all wrong. There were a lot of muscular, gay body builders, though. The paint job and the pristine upholstery on the benches appealed to the prim aesthetic of these men. They also got along very well with the gym receptionist. These guys were the ruling class in the gym. Bigger than anyone, there were more of them. They were skilled communicators, making strong, non-threatening eye contact in conversation, remembering and using people's names. And they always had a towel. They were the self-appointed ambassadors of the establishment. In the time I used the gym I never saw anyone resist the palm squeezing, gentle siren song of these solarium-bronzed giants.

When they talked among themselves, the topics were skin care, weight routines, new restaurants and approaching dance parties. When they talked with someone outside their circle they always, and with great skill, diversified the topics. So it was that they knew about my kung-fu practice and the machinations of other people's boardrooms and lunch halls. They were not, however, pure of humour or mind. There was no mistaking what was being discussed when they were all gathered and talking and looking at one or another young man training alone on a machine. One day when I was stretching after a session, rolling over the back of my shoulders, my legs behind my head, a mischievous and evenly modulated voice whispered in my ear, 'So, can you suck your own dick?'

In my shock, I straightened up too quickly and my back seized up. I needed Gianni's help to get down the stairs and had to miss three days' training.

The boys did give fantastic advice on gym training and their bodies stood testimony to their accumulated knowledge. They explained the importance of rest and tsk-tsked when I told them how much kung-fu training I was doing. They printed out sample diets and weekly menus for me. I listened when they discussed which supplements would best suit my needs and I blushed as they doted over my bench press. They joked about me being the city's nicest bouncer and asked when was the last time I slapped some poor unsuspecting thing.

The boys even visited me at work. They were warming up to a big night out and wanted to see me in uniform, they said. They were all immediately enamoured of Alby, his soft white skin and firm, resolute features. His self-assuredness and powerful posture had the boys fawning. Alby handled this charmingly.

In the midst of this, one of them said to me, 'Why do you do this when you are so obviously terrified?'

'I'm not terrified,' I said, stunned. I thought my fear had long since disappeared.

'You, my pretty, are shaking in your rather daggy boots.'

'It's just bad for my image to be talking to a bunch of poofs on duty.'

I had meant it as a deflection. It came out venomous and bitter. The troops were called to heel and left.

But they were right. Although I looked more the part – I had put on weight and was doing around ten hours a week of kung fu with Alby – I spent my nights on a knife edge of adrenalin and fear.

'They left in a hurry,' Alby noted.

For months, Alby had been trying to find a place of his own away from the city and all the karate boys. A place where we could train every day. And here it was. A huge red-brick church hall fifty metres long and thirty wide. Crumbly old floorboards stained with pigeon shit. It had none of the polish of the city and Alby loved it that way. We trained every weekday, with Saturday sessions in the park nearby and Sunday a day of rest.

All the students who had attended class in the city dropped off except me, the Vietnamese kid, and Lee. With a little advertising and word of mouth, the classes grew quickly. Lee and I found ourselves teaching the basics to groups of beginners and developing a healthy competition ourselves.

Lee was four years younger than me. Prodigiously athletic, he looked like a Staffordshire bull terrier: compact, hard and happy. He did things faster on sedatives than most people could on stimulants. Alby and I joked that we were just lucky Lee was a stoner – heaven forbid he should clean up his act and start embarrassing the two of us. My only real advantages over Lee when it came to open sparring were the length of my limbs, the extra classes I did and his deference to me. When we fought, it was essential for me to keep him at a distance. If the fight closed in and we traded body shots, I was lost. The power he generated in short punches was devastating.

On Saturday mornings we would meet an hour before the rest of the class arrived at the park. Sometimes we ran through the forms together. These were sets of fighting movements threaded together and taught as students progressed. Sometimes we drilled a particular technique, one of us attacking over and over while the other refined the preferred response. Most days though, we just beat the shit out of each other. And loved it. Lee broke my ribs and I broke his. We wore thin gloves and rarely stopped to refine technique. Testosterone flowed between us and we bonded more tightly than brothers in a dangerous primitive male dance. In the cool shade of the big elms, on the dew-moist grass we would tangle ourselves together and level one another with the hardest punches and kicks we had. Usually we limped away from these sessions, thighs violet with rising welts, torsos dappled in stinging pink blotches that would bruise by afternoon. Steam rose from our torsos, wet with shared sweat as we drank long from water bottles and pulled on T-shirts. These sessions were an open secret from Alby. He said he didn't approve, but we knew that he loved our enthusiasm and didn't want to run a 'soft' martial arts club. I rang Lee one day as I drove home to exclaim that I couldn't grip the steering wheel because my forearms were cramping from being pounded against his and he screamed with glee that he couldn't control his fingers.

Chapter 9
IMAGINE THE WORST

Friday night. Outside was hot and heavy. Signed on, greeted staff and manager, grabbed a stool on the way and sat myself next to Alby. He looked unmoved by my arrival. I was learning not to take his manner personally.

'New boots?' he asked.

'Yep. Bought 'em today.'

'Steel capped?'

'Yep.'

'Good-o.'

My bouncer look was complete. I was as close to a carbon copy of Alby as I could be. Black jeans, black T-shirt, black sweater, black jacket, number on my chest, qualifications in my pocket and now black steel-capped boots. My head had been shaved for a while now and I was putting on weight from my sessions in the gym. I didn't tell Alby, but I had even found a belt buckle almost the same as his – an enamelled cast-steel dragon that roiled around itself and held up my pants.

Alby was my teacher in martial arts and in bouncing. He taught by doing and I learnt by simulating. If I stuck at it, hardened myself, trained, persisted, I might one day be the sort of effective, efficient bouncer he was.

The staff had spotted my infatuation and poked fun at me. It was funny. We looked silly, little and big, young and old bouncers on either side of the door in identical clothes with matching shiny stubbly heads. But what did they know? They weren't at risk. They didn't have to fight or drag drunks out from under tables while the crowd jeered.

'Stop him.'

'Who?'

'Him. Coming in.'

'Outside?'

'Shit. Watch it.'

In my hesitation a man in his middle fifties, drunk and disorientated, was halfway through the door.

'No way, mate.'

Alby scooted around me, the door and the guy. He gripped the back of the man's pants at the belt and his right arm at the elbow. Even as the man turned his head to say something he was ejected back out onto the street, with the door shut in his face, muffling his yell.

'Oo ugin uvavugas. I vugin kill ou.'

He kicked one of the glass panels in the door, hard.

Alby opened the door like a falling guillotine and pushed his right foot straight out into the man's chest. Wind wheezed out of the man as the kick sent him reeling onto his bum in the middle of the pavement. The door shut and Alby sat down again. The guy collected himself, shuffled about holding his sternum and wandered away into the night.

'Do you think that was a bit rough?'

'No way. The managers don't like it but we're not here to make them happy. We're separate to the rest of the staff. It kills 'em that we sit around, most of the time, drinking tea and talking to customers, but soon as someone doesn't pay their bill or tries to touch the barmaid's arse they don't hesitate to ask us to jump in.'

'Mmm.'

'Cunts like that … dunno why they get so pissed, just asking to get bashed.'

We chuckled and looked out across the crowd. Smoke was gathering. The light was yellow, thrown off the shellac-coated walls, and the air was warm now from bodies and breath and the evening creeping in the open doors. The bar staff were soldier ants bent mutely to their tasks and the customers stood grazing in bovine groups, shoulder to shoulder across the floor. The noise of voices had risen until all that could be heard of the music was the far-off thunder of the bass speaker. Alby and I stood in silence for over an hour. Nothing remarkable happened. He leant against his stool. I shifted my weight occasionally from right to left and we avoided eye contact with customers who came and went.

'Do you get scared?' I said.

'Hey?'

'Scared on the job?'

'We're all just uppity monkeys mate. We eat, shit, masturbate and pound our chests to get a root or show off to the next big fella in sight. We've evolved to sniff out vulnerability and to capitalise on it. You can't afford to stand around this place being scared.'

So not even on the nights you're here alone? I'm scared from the moment I wake up on a day I gotta work.'

'Try visualising.'

'What?'

'Imagine yourself controlling situations. See people respecting your authority and listening to you. See yourself controlling people. Right?'

'Mmm.'

'If a guy scares you, imagine him attacking you. Think of different things he might do.'

'Uh, huh.'

'Then think of your reaction. Play dirty, kick him in the nuts, pull his hair, gouge his eyes. If you have to, you bite some guy's ear off. That should be something you have visualised already. Get it?'

'I think so. Is that what you do? Is that what you're doing when you stare out at the crowd?'

'No. I used to. A lot. Then you have a few fights, beat a few guys, nearly get done a few times and it's not as important. You relax.'

'Right, but it helps, yeah? It works?'

'Well, they usually do something you haven't thought of before, or the guy you're busy preparing for isn't the one who jumps you … but it does help.'

'Right. I'll try it.'

Alby told Lee and me at training that he wanted us to enter a kung fu competition. There would be three aspects to the competition. The first was forms, where competitors perform the movements particular to their style of kung fu and are assessed on agility, coordination and control. Second was point sparring where competitors face up against one another and, without attempting to actually hit the opponent, try to show their ability to outmanoeuvre them, displaying an option for striking – pulling the punch as close to the opponent as possible. When done satisfactorily or without too much contact, the fight is stopped and competitors return to starting positions. The third part was a three-minute round of unimpeded sparring. This sounded most like the way we trained with Alby. Unlike the points competition, this allowed light kicks below the waist and some contact. If the contact became excessive, the round would be suspended.

I trained for an extra half hour after class with Alby and Lee joined us when he could. Neither of us had seen one of these competitions before. I tried to push the memory of my earlier judo competition from my mind. Alby trained us as hard as ever, demanding that we punch and kick through the techniques with as much power as possible, saying it would be easier to hit softer on the day than to increase the intensity. If we left a hand down following a punch, Alby would swipe his pad hard into the space and knock our head this way or that, or leave a soccer-ball sized red welt against our ribs. He grunted at us to extend our arms and legs to full reach while maintaining power. It was exhausting and exhilarating. Alby didn't use any hierarchy or belt system so progress was not always clearly marked. Both Lee and I felt we were being pushed to a new level, and the extra attention from our teacher added to our sense of being groomed.

The competition was in a vast basketball complex. We arrived at eight thirty in the morning as instructed and sat through three hours of competition between under-twelves. The first competition round was the forms. We sat in huddles being called one by one to perform our little choreographed sequences. Most competitors seemed to have focused their training on speed and acrobatics. Alby had concentrated on martial application and a sense of strength. Lee and I were in different groups. We looked nervously across the hall at each other but we both did well and won our events.

Next was the point sparring. My competitor, who was a little taller than me and definitely weighed more, stood opposite. We bowed. The referee called, 'Fight'. The opponent came at me and punched straight. I feigned left to the outside of his extending arm, patted it out of the way and rammed my right hand into his exposed ribs. Only as he crumpled away did I remember that I should have pulled the punch. The referee warned me sternly that I would have to curb the contact or be disqualified. I tried. I beat the first opponent, and the second. The third bout amounted to a semi-final – the winner going into the final. The crowd was starting to make noise and the competitors were looking more and more serious. When the referee called, 'Fight', my opponent, a wiry, dark, young man, came rushing at me. As Alby had trained me to do, I stepped left and again let go a punch into the passing ribs. The opponent collapsed, the referee's whistle blew and my friends in the crowd cheered. I looked up and across to the other mat to see an unsuspecting young man take a silly risk on Lee's left hook. He threw a wayward right hook of his own. Lee ducked away and as he came up again, landed a left hook on the opponent that lifted him off the mat. The boy collapsed. Lee looked apologetically at him and then across at me. We were both disqualified, but we felt great. Sure we had broken the rules and been kicked out, but the training had paid dividends. Our technique and our reflexes were starting to function symbiotically. It translated into a sense of confidence that we could carry into the outside world, not just the rule-clad world of martial arts nerdiness.

Chapter 10

THOU SHALT HAVE BALLS

I WAS GETTING USED TO THE CHALLENGING STARES MEN THREW AS MY EYES passed. But no one had ever persisted like this before. Whenever I looked at him, he was looking at me. I was unnerved. The man was unremarkable. Early forties, shots of grey through his hair, a bland leather jacket and jeans. He was a touch shorter than me but would have weighed a lot more.

Every time I looked past his area of the room I could see him looking at me. I checked in my peripheral vision: there he was. I looked directly at him: there were his pinched, drunken eyes. I watched the people on my left and right as they came and went – it wasn't them he was looking at. There was nobody behind me. I was standing against a wall. I could see no grudge he should bear me. I concluded that I was the object of his scorn for no reason other than my position.

The guy had been staring at me for half my shift. I began to hold his stare. Sometimes he looked away, and sometimes he continued to look at me. His expression would not change. He gave no sign that he knew I was staring back at him.

'Hey, Alby, can you see that guy, grey hair, leather jacket?'

'Which one?'

'The one over there looking at me.'

'Yep, yep. I see him. What about him?'

'He keeps staring at me. Whenever I look at him, he's staring at me. I don't know him. Can't think why he's doing it. Do you know him?'

'Nuh. He's here all the time. Looks like a dickhead.'

I went back to my stool. Cigarette smoke hung above the crowd. The bar staff were all serving three or four drinks a minute. There must have been two hundred people in the bar alone and all I could see or think about was this guy who was still looking at me. I wanted it to stop. I asked Alby, 'What do you do? When someone just keeps staring at you?'

I looked at the guy. He was looking at me. I saw him smirk as he turned away. He was laughing at me. He could tell he had me worried. He could see me asking my mate for help.

'If it's bugging you, go and ask him what's so bloody interesting.'

'Really?'

'Yeah! If it shits you.'

'Right.'

Alby was good at making terrifying things seem perfectly ordinary. Problem was, when I was on my own, I was terrified once more. And there he was, still looking at me, and I imagined I could hear him saying to himself or his friends or me, 'Little bouncey-wouncey needs his big bad boss man to help him.'

The whole crowd heard him too, and turned around. They forgot their drinks and their cigarettes. They stopped trying to get laid and forgot about their bowls of chips. In unison, they all began to sing and stalk around me.

'Bouncey-wouncey is a weakling, bouncey-wouncey has no balls, bouncey-wouncey's got no dash.'

And in front of the massing, demonic crowd was the guy laughing and jeering at me.

'You're weak, mate. Weak, weak, weak, weak.'

I snapped out of my nightmare. The crowd was back to normal, back to their drinks and snacks, but the man was still looking at me. I got off my stool and moved towards him through the crowd. I lost feeling in my legs. I was floating, driven on only by the momentum of having started out towards him. He had seen me coming. I couldn't turn back now, though I wanted to. I got closer to him. My mouth was dry and I had no idea what to say. He turned to face me directly, challenge in his eyes.

'What are you looking at?' I said. It came out as a question instead of the cold-blooded threat I'd wanted.

'What?'

'What the fuck are you looking at, mate?'

This exploded from my mouth, spit as well, spraying him and surprising me. He leant back a little. Suddenly I felt unstoppable.

'Nothin', mate.'

'That's not what it bloody looks like. You haven't taken your eyes off me in two hours or more. Something you want to get off your chest?'

'No, you're right, mate, just thought you were a little … little.'

'I'll give you little, cunt. I'll take strips off you till there's nothing fuckin' left.'

I jabbed my finger into his chest.

'Look at me again and I'll beat you in the street. Got it?'

'Got it.'

I walked back to my stool. Every step expecting to feel his pot glass come down on the back of my head. I sat down. My body was quivering. The colour was draining out of my face. Alby smiled at me.

'Think you got your point across?'

I looked towards the guy. His back was turned to me, one of his mates was keeping lookout over his shoulder.

'Guess so.'

'Turned your back a little quickly.'

'Right.'

Nerves calming, and a feeling of power came over me. I felt ten-foot tall and bulletproof. I felt wild and unpredictable. I was no longer transparent. I took no shit. I drew lines in sand. I was a Bouncer.

Chapter 11

DARTH AND LUKE

'How are ya, Heath?'

'Yeah. Good, thanks. Ben?'

'Yep.'

'How are you?'

'Good, thanks.'

I showed Ben where to sign on and find a number, where to stash his coat, wallet and left him to get ready. He was my age or a little older, dark haired, my height and a little broader in the shoulder. He moved well, smooth and fluid.

I waited by the end of the bar, close to the front doors, where the staff made bottle-shop transactions. It was a crossroad between the restaurant, the bar floor, behind the bar and the stairs to the toilet and manager's office. Mabel, real name Anthony, hurried up to me from around the corner where Ben was signing on.

'Heath, who is that hunk around the corner? Please tell me he will be working here.'

'Ben. He's working here while Alby is away this weekend.'

'Just this weekend? Say it isn't so, oh, please.'

'He's going to be our back-up, coming in when someone else can't. I guess he'll eventually pick up some permanent shifts.'

'Oooohh, wait till I tell the girls. He is absolutely divine.'

'Don't scare him off. We've been trying to find someone to work casually for ages.'

'Scare him off? You're joking, aren't you? Is he gay?'

'That's what I mean! He's a very nice guy, I'm told. I know I'm jumping to conclusions, but he's working as a bouncer, his hair is a little ruffled and his T-shirt is creased ...'

'... give us time, sweetie.'

'But, Mabel, what about me? Thought we had something going here?'

'You're a sweetie, but him, well, let's just say he's Han Solo to your Luke Skywalker.'

I wanted to be Han, bad. I wanted to be edgy and enigmatic. But Mabel was right. My qualities were friendliness and curiosity.

I might have felt threatened by Ben, bigger than me, commanding, confident – but I wasn't. He felt like a brother.

'How was bouncer school?' I asked.

'Bit of a joke, really.'

'Same here.'

Ben didn't say anything. He did this a lot, if there was nothing for him to respond directly to, no question posed, he would remain silent, staring at you patiently. It was disquieting. Just when I was sure I was boring him I would say something about insecurity or nerves, or a dog I had seen on the street and he would break into a deep laugh.

'So, how did you end up working here?' I asked.

'I live down the street from Alby. We figured out we both did a martial art and got chatting. I'd been meaning to get my security licence for a while but nothing had given me that extra push. How 'bout you?'

'I started training with Alby about eighteen months ago. One day he told me there was some work going here … that was it. Do you do anything apart from train?'

'I'm a musician. You?'

'I tell myself I'm an artist. A painter. But for a while now all I've done is occasionally stand in my studio before or after training, maybe move a few things around.'

'Yeah, my training tends to take precedence lately over my music.'

'I guess the guys you meet in bands don't necessarily understand your need to finish early on Friday so you're fresh for Saturday training.'

'Shit, no.'

Conversation generally flowed easily between us. We were both obsessed with our martial art, both clinging to threads of an arts practice. The hours of the night flew by as the bar heaved around us. It was a nice change to talk to someone at work.

Though I was the senior security staff member it didn't feel that way. He was calm and unflustered, so when I spotted a man slumped on his bar stool holding a half empty glass and trying to roll a cigarette, I suggested Ben go and ask him to leave. He happily did. I watched him ask the man three times to leave, patiently listening to the man's friend who was asking for leniency. After a few minutes I got off my stool and walked to the bar. I stood behind Ben and listened. The evictee was dribbling words in his own defence down the front of his shirt, and his friend was imploring Ben to see the sobriety of the man.

I leant past Ben, grabbed hold of the slumped drunk and dragged him from his stool. He fell heavily to the ground, attracting the attention of people standing nearby. His friend pushed past Ben and lunged into me. We nearly fell together towards the door. This wasn't what I intended. I wanted to offer decisive support to Ben, not inflame the situation. Too late. The friend, blond and young, was yelling at me and pushing me. The crowd parted behind me and he held my shirt. Just as I was going to hit the wall I spun around, and my attacker, surprised, was thrown hard into the wall. Air whizzed from his lungs and he went limp.

I led him by his sleeves towards the door a metre to our left. He came to life and again we wrestled. Now we were outside, he had torn a sleeve from my jacket and our arms were intertwined, each of us holding the other's collar. Around the corner from the pub's front door, away from the noise and light, I could see his face above his white T-shirt – angry, scared, red. He let go with his right hand and pulled back his right shoulder. I released both my hands as he threw the haymaker. I deflected it with my left hand and – though I knew even in that shard of sweaty time I shouldn't – I punched him hard in the nose with my right hand. Turning him so his back was against the pub wall, I punched him again. His head snapped back and thudded into the wall. I punched again, up and into his right eye. His face was turned away from me. I punched again into his left jaw. Again the sound of his head against the wall. He turned and looked at me, pleading with his eyes. I held his shirt and listened to the soggy sound of my right hand punching his nose, again and again. He grunted and pulled at me, then pushed and tried to turn away but the momentum of my attack was controlling him. I couldn't hear the noises that usually filled my nights – the rush of cars, shoes scuffling, chat, laughter. We were in a quiet, violent tunnel and I was going to beat him to death.

'OK, OK. Leave it, fucking leave it!'

Ben jumped in front of me and separated me from my victim. The man whose face was now bloody and swollen tried to jump at me. Ben stayed between us as I tried to reach past and attack again.

'Do you want more, cunt, really?'

'Leave it, Heath! Jesus, fucking look at him!'

'Alright, alright.'

Ben pushed the man away, told him to piss off and I went inside. I was shaking from the adrenalin. My knees wobbled. The drunk man who had been the catalyst was hunched and sleeping against the outside wall of the pub where Ben had left him. My right hand was swelling and sore. My jacket hung in shreds from a shoulder and another man's blood was on my shirt. Ben stayed at the door making sure the man didn't return. I sat on my stool and looked around the bar. Faces turned away as my eyes crossed them. People looked at me like I was a wild animal, glanced sideways and looked at the floor. Flecks of spit were drying at the corners of my mouth and when I wiped them away, I smeared blood from my knuckles across my cheek. Ben joined me at the stool and I asked, 'He gone?'

'Yep.'

'Did he look alright?'

'Not really, but he left on his own two feet. Why don't you go clean up?'

'Yeah, yeah. I better go and write that in the incident register.'

'I reckon.'

When I saw my face in the toilet mirror, I was shocked. My eyes were wild, the pupils pinheads and the whites showing like little moons. Blood was streaked across my face like half-dried war paint. My jacket was torn from the collar all the way to the wrist. Surrounded by vats of cleaning product and boxes of toilet paper I splashed my face, threw the jacket in a bin and sat against the clothes dryer. Nausea and shock washed over me. I felt disgusting, dirty and invincible. The hum and rumble against my back was soothing, and let me relax. I didn't want to return to the bar. I didn't want to know if the police were there or if the man was dying in the street. Or if I had lost my job.

Something had happened inside me. From tonight, I would never be the same. I had tasted something simultaneously repugnant and intoxicating. Physical power.

It took twenty minutes to stand up. When I did my knees buckled and I bent over the bowl to vomit. I wretched a few times but nothing came up, save a long sticky line of shiny spit. I sat by the bowl waiting for another round of retching.

Alby made violence seem commonplace and unremarkable. I saw now that to be so calm about it must take great resolve. I saw the rhetoric used – 'some cunts are just askin' for it' – as a process of rationalisation. Some bouncers do it overtly, by posturing, while others do it quietly, internally. All of us have to find a way to accept that sometimes we are violent, and to set limits on that violence. If violence is part of your work, you have to have a working relationship with your aggression, or you are at its mercy.

I stood again and steeled myself. My legs found their strength. I looked once more in the mirror and went back to the bar. It had returned to normal, the crowd drank, smoked and chattered. Staff hurried about making drinks and collecting glasses. I sat down again next to Ben.

'Sorry about that mate, I should have left that longer, for you to resolve, made the whole thing go to shit …'

'No worries. Part of the job, eh?'

'Yeah, of course.'

I wished that I had said that.

I wanted to be righteous and assured like Alby, to let my actions speak and not feel they needed qualifying. But I wasn't. However, beneath my anxiety, glee was growing. After so many months as the trainee, it had happened. The fight. The violence.

Until now, I hadn't been in the middle of major physical confrontation. But now, I'd had been in the thick of it. Maybe I had lost my cool, but by primitive, tribal rules I had staked my claim over this square of hunting ground.

Ben and I continued to get along. We didn't work together very often, but we stayed in touch. We met occasionally to train in the park. Ben was a better martial artist than me. He had more control, more technique, more patience. I was fitter than him and a little more crazy. He almost always beat me on all levels. He hit me more, blocked and parried more of my attacks, had more energy left at the end of the session, had better drills to share with me. He had been training three years longer than me and had learnt that technique will always beat aggression. It was Alby's way to train for intensity and aggression. I lacked these qualities when I started with him.

Training with Ben showed me I now brimmed with them. Years later I would find new teachers who slowed me down, taught me patience and the value of correct technique.

One day, we were sparring in a dusty square of unkempt community lawn in the middle of nearby commission flats. We agreed to let our fight continue if we went to ground. Both of us did styles of martial art that only touched briefly on wrestling. Being on the ground was foreign to both of us. I had no memory of my years in judo. When we did hit the ground Ben lay over me and had me controlled. He put his forearm across my throat and as I started to struggle for air a couple of locals leaned out over their porch and screamed, 'Fuckin' kill him, mate. Kill the cunt and we'll give ya a drink, mate. Hahahaha!'

I was scared, and I was beaten. Ben weighed more than me and I couldn't throw him off. I was starting to see stars. I don't know how but I got his forearm between my teeth and without thinking, I bit him. He didn't remove his arm so I bit harder. Still he didn't relent, and then I felt the fibrous pop of my teeth breaking through his skin. My mouth felt salty like water at the sea and saliva started to fill my throat. Ben let go and looked at this arm.

'Sorry, mate.'

'No, you're right, you were turning purple. Good solution.'

Ben put his T-shirt over his arm and we walked back to his place. Crossing the last street before home he smiled.

'You bit me!'

'Sorry, again.'

'No worries.'

We trained together again after that and he continued to beat me. We were closer friends for the fights we had than I was with people I'd known for ten years. We held a silent respect for each other that was literally born of blood and sweat.

A week or two later, Alby said to me at work. 'Saw Ben in the street.'

'Oh yeah?'

'Told me you bit him.'

'Yeah, I did. Did he seemed pissed off about it?'

'No. Seemed impressed.'

'Oh.'

'You bit him, eh?'

'Yep.'

'You guys get on? You mates?'

'Yep.'

'And you bit him?'

'Yep.'

'Good on ya.'

CHAPTER 12
ANEFTERIOS

IT IS IMMEDIATELY APPARENT WHY SOME GUYS ARE BOUNCERS. THEY ARE genetically predisposed – smiling Polynesians the size of islands, Greeks with necks that start in their pockets, Albanians with leather jackets and shady friends, Aryian giants with pectorals like dinner plates. These guys were born huge. They came out of the womb in size ten shoes and tore their mother from arsehole to breakfast.

Others made themselves huge – steroid freaks with overblown foreheads and pimply backs. They would struggle to get up a staircase in a hurry but pin on a number, stand them by the door and everyone knows what they're there for.

Born or made, they're all hard to move with a truck.

I'm not one of these men. People don't take one look at me and then look again to see the other half. They never guess I'm a bouncer when they meet me at a party. Ever. When I tell people they don't believe me. But I had come to understand that being big did not make you unbreakable.

I worked, for one shift only, with a guy who was six foot six. He looked like a genetic experiment. An Aryan hulk. His name I don't remember but the view up to his nostrils across his pecs remains crystal clear.

It was the annual street parade. We were at the door of the Royal, while thousands packed the street. Stages were set up and people carried plastic buckets of beer. Eight guys were on shift and I was partnered with this blond monster.

A small man, perhaps on a drunken dare, leaped out of the crowd and punched my partner. It was unprovoked. We were taken by surprise. The fist landed on his throat. It wasn't a hard punch and I didn't even think to look at the big guy. The assailant turned around and was trying to return to the throng. I kicked him in the middle of the back as he disappeared into the crowd. I turned to my mate.

'Arsehole. You right?'

He stood stoically in position, his 'I'm fine' betrayed by two teardrops behind his sunglasses. He went to the toilet and without a word to me signed off, left work and was never seen again.

After four months at the Royal with Alby and working out at the gym, I felt more comfortable. I'd gained a few kilos and had been doing kung fu for a year. I was no Bruce Lee but I didn't feel as pathetic as I had on those first nights. I always worked with Alby, but now he was changing his shifts. On Saturday nights I would be working with Anefterios.

This guy was dressed from head to toe in black – shiny shoes, loose pants and a very tight T-shirt, a chunky gold necklace around his neck and a collection of weighty rings on his right hand. 'Terry?' I asked.

'Yeah, mate.'

'I'm Heath, I'm working with you tonight.'

'Yeah, guessed by the number on your shirt, mate.'

Terry was the biggest man I had ever stood next to. He made the Aryan hulk look like my kid sister. Terry's biceps were as big as my thighs. I actually measured my thighs after he told me the circumference of his arm. Anefterios was a towering bouncer god in whose shadow we all scurried about in awe. I had no hope of ever being like him. I was just lucky he was on my team.

He had worked in the days before regulation, when teams of men were hired without formal employment, no names were submitted and they were answerable to no one. And here he was working with me, seventy-five kilograms of well intentioned, middle-class, qualified teacher with a year of kung fu under my belt.

'You know you're not gonna get any real trouble here. Any place gets real trouble, you can tell 'cos the tables and chairs are bolted to the floor. Nothin's served in glass – there's usually a blood kit in the drawer. Only people who are gonna cause any trouble here are Greeks and Lebos, and most of 'em know me, so it's awright.'

'Are you Greek?' His face suddenly changed. I thought I was about to die. Then he smiled.

'Never ask a Maco if he's Greek. Where your parents from? England?'

How feeble. How colourless. How pale it suddenly was, to be English–Australian.

'Yeah. What's your real name?'

'Anefterios, mate. Anefterios Jolevski.'

Anefterios had grown up in the housing commission flats up the street. He had been hitting people since he was twelve, when he won his first kickboxing championship. He made a living as a bouncer and kickboxing coach. He had eighteen years of working as a bouncer in the biggest, nastiest venues in town behind him.

Terry opened the door for people. I presumed it was a courtesy until the time he opened the door and it froze in its swing. The entering patron bumped into the glass.

'Na mate, had too much.'

The man looked up. His eyes passed over Terry's biceps. He quietly turned and left. Opening the door to people wasn't servitude. It was a tool of control. Terry's size, jewellery, battered face and manner did the job. When I told someone to leave, I just waited until they looked over my shoulder at Terry. Then they did just what I said.

Terry could talk the bottom off a barstool. He said to me one night, 'So ya do kung fu, eh, grasshopper? S'pose it's good for a guy your size. Whad'ya practice? Lots of eye pokes and ball grabs?'

'Yeah, some.'

'Loves that stuff, Alby does. I did kung fu for years. Me and me mates used to watch the films, and we'd just learn it from there. We were sick, mate. This was before it was big, mate. In the late sixties, early seventies, when were you born. Yeah, too late, mate. You're too late, mate. The good flicks were in the drive-ins, double features. We'd go down there and climb the fence and copy the moves while they were on the screen. I was smaller than you then. Shit, we learnt it all. None of the good stuff's on video these days, mate. Never got there.'

Relief. I knew more about early kung fu films than anyone. I could talk with Terry as an equal. I listed some of the more seminal films and fight scenes. He simply talked over the top of me.

'They're all shit. Nothing compared to the good ones: *Snake in Eagle's Fist*, *Nine Mighty Warriors of Shaolin*, *Shaolin's Last Days*.

I had seen them, and he was right, they were crackers, but they weren't the best. But what I thought clearly didn't matter.

'What you gotta do, right, is travel round to all the video stores out in Preston and Fawkner, all the real woggy ones, you'll find top collections.'

Suddenly, two men were fighting at the far end of the bar. Noise erupted through the pub and the two of us raced over. Moving through the crowd was easy. I followed Terry. Patrons skittled aside as he ploughed through the crowd. Like Obi Wan Kenobi, I heard Alby's words, 'Keep your chin down and make a lotta noise.' A circle had formed around the fighters, jeering and chanting. I put my chin down and yelled. I was right behind Terry, screaming like a banshee as we approached the two brawlers. They were wrestling with each other trying to find space to swing punches.

Without word or hesitation Terry punched the closer man in the side of the head. His head bounced from one side to the other and his body went limp beneath him. The crowd was silenced. My war cry continued some seconds too long. Terry stood over the unconscious man and said to the remaining fighter, 'Pull your fuckin' head in.'

The man shrank. The man Terry had hit was lying on the ground staring up, his eyes glassy. I was frozen.

Terry shunted me aside and grabbed the prone man by the back of his collar. Like a cartoon cave man, he dragged the man back through the bar to the door. The crowd noiselessly parted before him and stared as he passed. I followed. Halfway along the bar the man came to and began shouting and struggling to stand. Terry's momentum was too great for the poor guy to get a footing. Terry opened the door and threw the man like a scrap onto the street. I arrived seconds later.

'That was an awful lot of noise you made back there,' he said. 'Doin' it for your highland ancestors mate?'

I felt small and pink and fragile.

If not for Terry, my security career might have finished there. I was offered a temporary position as a lecturer in my old ceramics department. It was a dream come true. Presenting my first week of classes, it was obvious that I was more naturally disposed to creativity and fostering inspiration in others, but there was no adrenalin and no danger. I enjoyed the thrill and uncertainty of a shift on the door of the pub more than I had realised. In my life outside bouncing, everything was measured in minute degrees. Marking students' mid-semester submissions, I struggled for diplomacy. The politics of a tertiary institution staffroom were beyond me. When I was with Terry or Alby, dangerous as it might be, at least the boundaries and roles were clear-cut and manageable.

Chapter 13
THE ALLSTARS

I'D MENTIONED TO TERRY THAT I WAS DOING WEIGHTS. WITH IMPRESSIVE diplomacy he had explained that 'the boys' at my gym might get me big, but they didn't know how to do weight training to complement martial arts training. He offered to write me a 'real' program, at his gym.

The gym was in a red brick building with no signage. There was no desk and no receptionist. All that told me I was in the right place was a sign above a stairway going down that read, 'Gloves and mouthguard must be worn beyond this point.' The cement underfoot was bare and cold. The stairs were unlit. I was guided not by light but by muffled shouts, thuds and the intermittent ringing of a bell.

Four flights down I heard the low splashy thuds of gloves striking flesh and the slapping claps of glove against pad. A bell rang. Clouds of old sweat shoved back up the stairs at me. I heard the machine-gun rattle of speedballs. Men's voices barked through the air and grunted in action. The whirring of powerful fans hummed like the din of a crowd.

Inside to my left was the boxing ring. It was raised a foot from the floor and covered in a worn, stained tarpaulin. The ring was five metres on each side with padded corner posts. Three cables hung between each post like the spines of old ponies.

Three men were in the ring. Two were in shorts, wearing puffy red gloves, high-ankled trainers and no shirts, moving round each other with their hands up round their heads. Torsos darted left to right in anticipation and response to their partner's attack. There were damp patches on the canvas from the drizzle of their sweat.

Moving around them, barking demands and being massive was Anefterios. He wore a loose T-shirt but still his pectorals cast a long shadow over his abdomen. Thirty kilos heavier than his charges, he moved just as freely. It was 'Swan Lake' danced by a bull elephant.

'WhadIfuckinsaydonstopmoveyafeetyourfuckinasleeponyourfeetkeep itgoinleftleftleftfuckinleftweaveyoucuntohmatecomeonwhereareyourcom binationsIcancountthepunchesbeforeyouthrowemyoufuckingirl.'

After three minutes a bell rattled. End of the round. Anefterios continued to berate the fighters.

'You're fuckin' girls, mate. What's wrong with you? Too much fuckin' round. You're not even trying to move. If you don't start moving your fucking feet I'll give you fuckin' brain damage, mate. And where's your fuckin' workload? Fuck! And what's with you, ya dim cunt? May as well put your fuckin' left hand in your pocket for all the use it's getting. Fact. Why not just put it back on your dick.'

The bell clattered and they started again. The boxers' gloves were slick and shining with sweat. They hit each other hard: jabs, hooks, right crosses, left leads, right leads, upper-cuts short and long. I knew the names of these punches but had never seen application like this. The strikes came off the young, tensile bodies like hailstorms. Their footwork was incredible. Tiny staccato steps quickly and fluidly beat out a jazzy, off-kilter tempo against the mat.

What they were doing was utterly different to kung fu. Alby taught a wide range of moves – ground fighting and kicking, joint locks and various hand strikes – but the boxers used only punches. Their finesse was astonishing.

Anefterios saw me. I must have looked absurd, leaning in the doorway, eyes huge with attention. He walked away from the fighters, leant onto the ropes and extended a hand.

'Hey, big man.'

'Hey, Terry. Am I too early?'

'No mate. Give us a minute and I'll be with you. Just finishing up with these guys. Have a look around. Bet it looks different to Alby's place.'

The space was huge, low-ceilinged and long. Square cement pillars ran the length of the room at equal intervals. On all four sides of each pillar there was a punching bag. Some were large, long sausage bags hung a foot or two out from the pillar, allowing them to swing when hit. Others were swollen upside down L-shapes that let the user practise punching up as well as straight. Some were simply cast-off car tyres bolted or strapped to the wall at about thigh height. At one of these posts, with a tyre in front of him, was a young Aboriginal man. He was fit, chiselled, glistening and ferocious. He kicked his shin against the tyre as hard as he could. Massive red welts shone down the front of each shin. With each kick he released a chilling scream of pain and aggression.

On other pillars hung speedballs. Three were hurtling back and forth in a haze of movement and noise, a hypnotic blur, pounded by young men whose hands rolled patty-cake, patty-cake in front of their eyes.

The unused ones dangled like the prolapsed nipples of a dog. Along one wall fans turned side to side like the floating heads of sideshow clowns. A low, wooden bench ran the length of the wall. Bags overflowing with cotton straps, gloves, drinks, bananas, towels, mouth-guards and sweaty shirts were shoved under it. The wall closest to me had a small area of floor-to-ceiling mirrors in front of a weight area. There were no cable machines. Just piles and rows of free weights, dumbbells and barbells. None of the benches were upholstered. Bare wood. Everything but the weights was bolted to the floor.

All available wall space was covered in memorabilia relating to boxing and kickboxing – photos, magazine clippings, newspaper articles, press portraits and action shots. There would be little room for a discussion of the merits of different schools of martial arts in this gym.

There were fading photos of men in the coy poses of old-time boxers. White men, browned by time and failing chemicals, poised and superior. More recent photos showed darker-skinned men. The shorts were bigger, and worn lower on the body, the hands closer to the face in defence. I only recognised the really famous ones: Tyson, Lewis and Spinks. But there were dozens more of smaller, swarthier men wearing championship belts. Latinos, Mexicans, Puerto Rican, Panamanian, Cuban. Handsome men with suspicious eyes.

After another few rounds with his charges, Terry took me into his shoebox office at the end of the gym. There were two decorations in the room. One was a photo of Anefterios, fighting fit, in classic boxer pose, shoulders hunched over his abdominals, elbows in tight against his ribs and chin down, close to his chest. It was a black and white photo and the lighting fell in a conspicuously flattering way across rippling muscles.

The other was an A3 photocopy hanging pathetically from one pin with black text: AS HARD AS YOU TRAIN, SOMEONE, SOMEWHERE, IS TRAINING HARDER.

Terry looked at the weight program I had brought.

'You've been using cable machines. FUCK ME. Don't you know anything?'

He tore up my program and tossed the pieces into the bin. Forget about calipers for assessing body fat, a blood-pressure gauge or a ten-minute heart-rate test. Anefterios measured my biceps, thighs, chest, waist and calves. He checked to see if I could touch my toes and took my pulse. He then wrote a weight and conditioning program. He took me into the gym, handed me a piece of thick plastic tubing with handles and instructed me to skip for ten minutes. I found myself a spot on the floor and tried to remember how to skip. I was still tripping over the rope on its first revolution when he yelled at me from halfway down the room.

'Take your fuckin' shoes off!'

Every time the tube hit my bare foot it raised a welt. In three minutes the tops of both feet were vivid red and stinging with pain. Fifteen minutes later, Anefterios strolled towards me, smiling.

'Had to add five minutes for all the time you spent with the rope around your ankles.'

I stopped skipping.

'Thanks.'

He walked me through the program he had written for me. Everything was free weights. I had to do five sets of every exercise, the last to be done until failure. That is, until I was physically unable to go on. He had me doing chin-ups, where I pulled myself upwards; dips, where I lowered myself down between two bars and lifted myself back up again; bench presses without the stabilising aid of cables and metal runners; squats with a loaded barbell across my shoulders and no support. Throughout every set of every exercise Anefterios stood over me.

'My ten-year-old nephew lifts more weight than this, big fella. Stop holding out on me. Give me all you've got. Don't be shy, mate.'

When I lay on the benches to lift weight his huge head would fill my vision and demand harder work.

'Chicken boy. That's what I reckon I'm gonna call ya. Hey, fellas. This guy's new name is "Chicken boy". Make sure you use it.' He saw the pain this caused me.

'Mate! "Chicken boy". In this place it's better than me telling a bunch of boxers you're the kung fu kid.' He winked and I had to trust him.

At the end of the lifts he supervised a fifteen-minute destruction of my abdominal wall and then said, 'Off you go. Grab a kebab on the way home. Get some rest and come back and do it again in two days, and every two days after that. Three times a week, get up early and run at least four k's. Tell Alby what I've got you doing and don't let him get carried away when he's training you. Oh, and tell him he's a softcock. HAH!'

It was ninety minutes since I had arrived at the gym. My body ached. There were bleeding welts all over the tops of my feet. Sweat ran off me in rivers and I was swallowing hard to stop myself crying or vomiting.

I walked fifteen blocks home, taking the back streets through Collingwood. Beneath my pain was a determination to return to the gym, rise to the challenge of the weights – and keep doing a job that scared and confronted me. After a long hot shower, and a kebab, I lay in my bed and cried, because I hurt, and because the hill I was starting up was high.

Chapter 14
REAL TIME

ONE NIGHT I WAS WORKING WITH ANEFTERIOS AT THE ROYAL. A MAN approached us, sweaty and swollen. Denim and bad leather boots. He leant into Terry's space and made small talk.

'What's your name buddy?'

'Na, mate, just number 38 to you.'

'Aw, come on mate, I'm Vern. I tell ya my name, you tell me yours. Fair trade, eh?'

'Have to be happy with a number. Go get yaself another drink.'

Terry and I were standing side by side against the wall, next to a door.

'Aw, come on, big boy. Tell us ya name. How you get so big anyway? Mama's cookin?'

'Yep.'

'Bullshit, mate.'

He was leaning on the wall next to Terry now.

'You do kickboxing or something, or you just a gym junkie?'

'Mama's cookin' like you said mate.'

Moving off the wall and standing in front of Terry again, Vern started to get cocky.

'Come on, what's your deal? You a fighter or a looker? My guess is you never had a fight in your life. You just go to the gym five times a week. Right?'

Vern was drunk. Or blind. Everything from Terry's nose to his neck said fighter.

'Answer me, big fella. Come on, you just watch your muscles grow in the mirror, don't you? I bet you pull yourself in front of it. Let's see your skills, mate. What ya got?'

The crowd around us was oblivious. Vern's weight shifted back, as he wound up a punch. Before his hand reached his ribs, Terry's left elbow swept up the side of his body, then cut down across Vern's jaw. Vern never saw it, or the floor when he hit it. Out cold. I was stunned. Terry had not shown the slightest agitation.

Two, maybe three people including me saw Terry's strike. By the time Vern was on the ground, twenty or more people were watching, intrigued.

I slapped Vern's cheeks and he stirred. Terry was inside the door looking over the bar. I stood Vern up and walked him out. He stared back at me all pain and crushed pride. The door swung shut in his face.

'Terry, that was amazing. You knocked him out cold!'

'Na, mate, just doin' the job. Sad prick.'

Vern returned to the door a little later, recharged. He stood outside, interrupting the flow of the sidewalk and calling Terry out to his death. Terry was oblivious.

My mother wasn't when she cautiously made her way past Vern and through the door.

'Mum, hi.'

'Hi. We thought we'd visit you, we're on our way to the Malthouse.'

'What's on, is it *The Tempest*?'

'Yes. We're hoping Bell is better in this than as Hamlet last year. Who is that man? Is he talking to you?'

'He's just some sad prick, and he's mainly talking to Terry. Mum this is Anefterios, Anefterios, this is my mum, Karen, and her partner Sally.'

'Ladies.'

'Aneefterryass,' my mother chimed awkwardly. Mum is much shorter than me, and slight. Moving into her sixties with flair and staying thin. Low-heeled shoes, short, angular hair and prominent earrings. She was tiny, looking up at Anefterios. She couldn't conceal her awe. Her eyes lingered in wonder over his swollen upper arms. Sally was more interested in Vern, who was still gesticulating aggressively outside the glass door. Mum followed Sally's gaze and asked, 'Do you get a lot of this sort of thing?'

I was about to say no, hardly at all, my job is perfectly safe Mum, but Terry answered. 'Pretty standard sorta bullshit. Sorry, mischief, for a Saturday night.'

'Oh,' Sally said.

Mum stepped closer, clasped my elbow and gently led me a step away from Terry, who looked out over the crowd.

'Sweetie, seriously, how long are you going to do this? What's wrong with teaching?'

'Mum. Not now. Why don't you just head over to Southbank for a drink, just somewhere else?' I hissed into her ear.

'OK, OK, we just wanted to drop in and see how you were. Shall we go, Sally? Aneefterrier, it was lovely meeting you. Do look after my son, won't you?'

'Of course.'

'Thanks. See you soon, Heath.'

She kissed me goodbye. Vern was still calling Terry and me 'stinking cunts' with his face pressed against the door.

'See ya, Mum. Use that door down there to get away from this guy, and enjoy the show.'

Mum and Sally negotiated their way through the crowd to the next exit.

Terry let some time pass before asking, 'What's your mum do?'

'Public service.'

'What's her business?'

'What business?'

'Her partner?'

'Life partner. They're life partners.'

'Life partners? They're lesos?'

'Yep. Lesbians.'

'Oh. So they fuck each other?'

'Pretty much. That's it, yep.'

Whatever credibility I had as a hard man just left with my mum and her life partner.

Chapter 15

YOU GOT NO DASH

'HEY, MAE, 'OW'S YOUR NIGH GOIN'?"

'Pretty good. Yours?

'The nighs alrigh buh the week was sheet. Worked all week buildin' fences in Cheltenham.'

'Weather wasn't really on your side.'

'You're tellin' me! Wind, rain, wind. Rain. Farck! Anyway, its Fridee, I'm fucked and now all I need's a root and ah'll be righ. Get to Fridee and all you wanna do is sink piss, sit on your arse and have some sheila suck your dick.'

'I work Friday and Saturday nights.'

'Course you do. You know what I mean, specially the blow job?'

'Absolutely. Scuse me, mate.'

Alby was looking studiously away from me and my moron. I crossed the doorway and stood next to him.

'You don't have to talk to them, you know.'

'How do you avoid it?'

'Anyway you can. Pretend you can't hear 'em. Ignore them.'

'So when you go off to look round the bar…'

'Just makin' a getaway mate.'

His eyes went to the door. 'Better ask for ID.'

Five men were at the door. Their skin was coarse from working long hours outdoors. Their shirts had matching logos on the pockets. Their hair was combed and parted like older men but there was youth in their eyes and posture.

I said, 'Evening, gents.'

They avoided eye contact and as they came in the door, only two of them returned my greeting.

'You guys got some ID?'

'Sure.'

One offered his card, but the other four moved quickly towards the back of the room. Alby got in front of them and herded them back to me.

I repeated, 'ID, guys.'

The first boy, who had proven his age, opened the door and stepped outside. Two others followed him. They knew there was no point continuing with their mission. The two boys still inside stood too close to me. They produced ID.

'Sorry, guys. Welding tickets won't do it. Need a licence or Keypass. Here you go, better join your mates outside.'

'Ar, carm on, may.'

'No ID, no drinks.'

'Yer shittin' me. Carn, may, you can turn a blind eye fer us mate, carnya?'

'Love to guys, but it's not worth my job. Cops find you in here without ID, it's my arse on the line.'

Alby was moving around my right side putting them between him and the door. They were oblivious.

'This place is fucked, and you, you cunt, your fuc…'

The door was still open and before the kid completed his expletive, Alby hoisted him by the belt of his pants out the door. The remaining boy took his cue and left. The five of them gathered on the doorstep and the vocal one started up again.

'You, little cunt, come out 'ere an I'll kick fuckin' tar out of you, ya fuckin' weak cunt.'

Alby stepped into the doorway.

'Not you, ya fat fuck, I want the small cunt, hidin' behind ya. Come on, cunt, I'll fuckin 'ave ya. Stop hiding behind your fat fuckin' mate 'ere. I wanna fuckin' shot a ya.'

People inside the bar had stopped and pressed up behind Alby and I for a look. Pedestrians on the street took a wide berth around the small gang clustered on our step. I was frozen. I wanted to jam my fist down his throat, but I didn't move.

'Arrr, ya got no fuckin' dash in ya, cunt. No dash, no go, mate, no guts, no spark, no farkin dash in ya, you weak cunt. I hate you, cunt. Fuck you and fuck your family.'

Alby shut the door.

The little welder's mates pulled him away and down the street. I watched his mouth, muted by the glass door, moving, throwing silent abuse at me. The crowd settled behind us. We sat down again and a few customers made jokes about how desperate for a drink the youth of today must be.

'Do you think I could have taken that guy?'

'What? He had nothing, all mouth.'

'How come you stood between me and them at the door?'

'Just 'cos you could beat em's no reason to have a fight. Never look for trouble, ever. Lesson from Bouncer school. Hotcocks like that, even after you knocked 'em down a rung are just as likely to come back with ten mates. If you can, always ignore 'em, tell 'em to piss off and shut the door. Swallow your pride.'

'OK.'

I opened the door and stood on the step of the pub. It put me a head higher than the pavement crowd. I liked this spot. I could survey the street, watch the traffic flowing through the junction. In this view people were always moving, always going somewhere. They moved in an orderly fashion, compared to the swaying mosh that the bar became after eight.

I half hoped the little welder would come back. My adrenalin had settled and I wanted to pound my chest. To show the world how far I had come towards bouncerdom, I took out my mobile and dialled Rachel.

'Hello? Rach. Yeah, it's Heath. What you up to tonight? You still working at the tavern? You are ... Surprised I haven't seen you more ... I'm working at the Royal ... Come past on your way into work. Haven't seen you for ages ... Cool see you then.'

It was two years since I'd seen Rachel. When she stopped by on her way to work I was still standing on my step watching the footpath parade.

'Oh. You're the bouncer. Fancy, there I was imagining you'd be pullin' lagers.'

'I've been doing this for a year or so.'

I crossed my arms over my chest and gently pressed my biceps back against me. The cotton sleeves of my Bonds T-shirt stretched gratifyingly against my skin. Rachel noticed and her look took in my arms.

'Wow. You been liftin' weights?'

'And training with Alby. Remember, you suggested it?'

'Yeah, I do. Didn't think you'd get carried away with it. God! You really have changed, you sort of look like … like a man.'

'Schucks. Thanks, Rach.'

Bingo. Rachel went off to work and I preened a little longer on my stoop. When I went back in Alby smiled and said, 'She impressed?'

'Eh?'

'She looked impressed. Haven't seen her for a while? Reckon you might be seeing a little more of her from now on.'

'Oh, no, we used to go out. Actually, she suggested I train with you.'

'She break it off or you?'

'Oh, you know, bit of both.'

'She seen you since you started training?'

'No.'

'Like I said, reckon you might start seeing a little more of her now.'

Chapter 16

MALE PATRON REMOVED FOR INAPPRORIATE BEHAVIOUR. NO FORCE USED.

SUNDAY TO WEDNESDAY NIGHTS THE SECURITY WORKED ALONE. USUALLY, THE bar had a smattering of couples and mates who weren't prepared to waste a weekend night on the other.

The bar was no more full than a regular Wednesday. But tonight there were no couples or quiet pairs of mates. The only people in the pub were twenty young men. A footy team, probably. Round after round of beer and the occasional dainty, dangerous line of tequilas. I asked them to stop singing Cold Chisel a couple of times. There were a couple of loud whispers about the dangerous-looking security guy.

Toilets for the general public were at the top of stairs that began at one end of the bar. There was a door onto the street at the foot of the stairs so people could enter the pub, use the toilet and leave without setting foot in the bar or restaurant. On a scale of one to ten for pub toilets, these were a stinky three or four. We used the clean, staff toilets except when we were on duty alone.

Close to eleven I went up for a piss. I warned the bar manager and climbed the stairs. Three men from downstairs were at the urinal leaning back slightly and looking over their shoulders to continue their conversation. They didn't adjust the tone or topic – whether the bar girl would spit or swallow. When I entered I was neither excluded from their discussion or included.

It is easy to forget the absurdity of pissing at urinals. We stand next to men we don't know and listen to them chat, or chat with them while we hold our cocks.

I stood at the urinal and one by one they packed up and waited for each other. None of them washed their hands. As my hushing arc of piss hit the stainless steel, the men began leaving the toilet. The second through the door paused, tilted his head and spat on the floor.

Alone, I considered this. He'd not spat at me, nor threatened me, but by the time my pants were zipped I knew I was going to throw him out.

I approached the group. I caught the eye of the bar. I circled the men until I was standing by the shoulder of the spitter. The slurred conversation slowed and before he could turn to face me I said, 'You're gonna have to leave, mate.'

'Why?'

'I'm not going to have you in here walking around spitting on the floor. Wanna behave like you're on the street, you may as well be out there.'

'What? Your jokin' aren't you?'

His friends told me to relax, to take it easy. They were just having a few beers. Everything was fine.

'You guys can stay but he's going. It's not negotiable. Let's go, please, mate.'

Faced with a pack issue, the 'leader' stepped towards me and began advocating his friend.

'Dono wot he did but I'll keep an eye on 'im an make sure he's alright.'

'Sorry, mate. He's gotta go.'

The leader stepped closer. I could feel his breath and smell its boozy fug. I didn't move. We stared at each other. I concentrated on seeming calm but my right heel was off the ground and my abdomen braced. After what felt like a week, he stepped back into the circle. I took my cue.

'Come on, mate. Out.'

Holding the inside of his elbow, I gestured for the spitter to leave. He started walking, saying boisterous goodbyes, promising to meet them at another bar. As he walked out the door he mentioned that he had fucked my mother recently. Once he was moving along the pavement, I went down the bar to the other door at the bottom of the toilet stairs. My foot against it stopped him opening it. He spat on the glass but continued down the street. I returned to the main door.

Later the group left the bar. I moved away from the door, leant on the stained hardwood bar and talked to the staff. In the ornately framed mirror over the bar I watched the football team file away from me, out the door and into the night.

At midday the following Saturday I was sitting next to Lee in the Edinburgh Gardens. He was impressed with my story of splitting a footy team from their mate, and for my strong ethical stance on public hygiene. We had been sparring. He had sore legs because I had been kicking them. I couldn't see, which was why we were sitting down. He'd scored a perfect ten with his elbow on the bridge of my nose. Blood ran down my nostrils through my hand and down my arm. Sweat and tears seared my eyes. We were laughing.

'Good start to the morning, mate,' said Lee.

'Yep, got up this morning and thought, what I need from today is two black eyes and a blood nose. And I know just the man …'

'Always a pleasure, mate.'

'Cheers. How was your Friday night?'

'Good. Just went out with some of the boys. Coupla bars. Ended up in this really cool little place in some laneway up the top of the city. Cocktail place. We were pretty sideways by the time we were there but I got talking to some guy behind the bar and he said they were after security. I told him I did kung fu and he offered me the job. But I can't take it without training can I?'

'Nuh. You'd have to do bouncer school. It's not too painful if you don't hope for too much.'

'Oh mate, I'm not really up for it. I'm not big enough to start with. You should do it. Specially after your effort with the footy team.'

'These flash-in-the-pan places. Flavour of the month stuff. The work's there for a year or two but they don't have any longevity.'

My deadpan delivery and the cynicism was a word-perfect quote from Alby.

'Well, I think I've got the guy's number. Let me know if you change your mind.'

'Cheers.'

The truth was that since my mum had visited me at work, I'd been wondering how long I could keep doing the job. I couldn't see myself in my late forties standing by the door of a pub like Alby. I got bored too easily. The less terrified I was of the work, the more bored I became. I sensed that my life needed to change direction.

Chapter 17
THE END OF THE APPRENTICESHIP

ALBY AND I WERE STANDING ON EITHER SIDE OF THE CORNER DOOR INSIDE THE Royal one Friday night. It was too busy and noisy to talk so we just watched the crowd and the doors. I treasured my Friday nights now as it was the only night I worked with Alby.

The street had worked up a good head of steam. Cars edged along slowly, drivers hoping impossibly for a park. Groups of people ambled up and down the strip. Autumn was giving way to winter and though it wasn't cold, the wind made people shudder when waiting for the lights. An old man with a dog as dark as a shadow shuffled by, a red bike light attached to its collar.

The crowds in the restaurants were starting to thin and cars with booming bass systems and immaculate duco were coming down the street headed for the Spanish section of the suburb.

Even though Alby and I had been working together for almost two years, I still felt very much a student. I'd thrown people out and I'd knocked a lot back at the door. I was able to clear the pub at the end of the night by myself and sometimes I escorted the manager upstairs with till trays when they were doing a clearance. Still, I knew that something was not entirely convincing. When I told people to do something they looked at the guy behind me. In time I would learn that this is not always a bad thing, but now, it just made me feel a fake.

I looked across the doorway to Alby. He sat on his stool lost, apparently, in thought, his back hunched. I could see out the doors. I had a good view. I could see most of the people that came to the main entrance.

A group of six or eight young men walked into view. Punks, in a seventies London way – torn denim, sleeveless leather, studs, spiky hair, chains, knee-high Doc Martens and facial piercings. They were moving slowly down the street, looking relatively peaceful.

The traffic lights turned red and two cars pulled up. One was an orange Charger, low to the ground with shining mag wheels. The car behind it was smaller. A turquoise Holden Gemini, also from the seventies. It bristled with exhausts and extractors. Little display dials jutted out from the bonnet like periscopes and the chassis vibrated to the subsonic bounce of the speaker in the boot. Both cars were carrying a full load of passengers.

One of the men in the Gemini yelled something at the punks, now in the middle of my window-frame view. Common Saturday-night stuff. One of the punks told the guy to go fuck himself and threw a bottle of juice at the car. He didn't realise that it wasn't a car but a supercharged, freshly painted, fully fuelled, four-cylinder fantasy. The glass hadn't reached the car before all four doors were open.

A crowd controller is obliged to try and control any situation that he can see from the boundary of his workplace. I wished we didn't have so many glass doors. I stood and slapped Alby's thigh, gesturing we go outside. I opened the door to see the four Gemini guys hurtling across the road. The five men inside the orange Charger were also crossing the road. Alby and I stepped from the pub to a small corridor of asphalt with eight punks on our left and nine swollen suburban Hispanics on our right. Other pedestrians on the pavement disappeared.

Without talking, we stood back to back as the two groups approached each other. One spiky, bright and white faced. The other swarthy, snarling and pretty. The groups collided around us.

I had never been in a brawl before. Sometimes at training Alby would set two or three people against one as an exercise, but you knew their names, that they were a pretty nice bunch of guys and that Alby was watching. Now, we were outnumbered five times over by guys we didn't know and no one was going to intervene. We weren't the target of either group, just an obstacle.

For the first few seconds I heard nothing as fists slammed into faces in both directions. When people fight like this, in the street, driven by stupid, base aggression, they always strike at the head first. Both sides try to out-muscle and out-punch the other. One of the men knocked into me and all the noise and swearing and violence of the situation became real. I heard the chinkling of chains and wet, cutting cabbage sounds of flesh and bone being pressed hard and suddenly against each other. I felt Alby's big back against mine and I tucked my chin to my chest, raised my shoulders and loosened the focus of my eyes. A body came at me from the left. Against a backdrop of staring faces behind the pub glass I bent my knees and drove my right arm straight out. He swung at my lowered head, my fist landed in his gut, he bent over and I threw him aside.

Pushing back against Alby I heard him telling everyone to piss off. My voice fired a warning squawk and then found its pitch in my belly. We yelled for everyone to 'fuck off'. Alby pushed back into me. I lowered into my hips and pushed out hard with both hands as a man's body was knocked into me. Pressed against each other Alby and I circled and screamed our way through the melee, using each other as ballast to deflect bodies and blows. As quickly as the fight had begun, the group separated. In their factions the men retreated from each other and left Alby and me standing together in the middle. Some of them had blood noses and swelling eyes, some shirts were ripped, but no one looked too bad. The car drivers walked back to their chariots and skidded the wheels furiously around the corner. The punks walked back the way they had come.

Alby and I returned to the bar. People inside congratulated us and patted our backs but we had nothing to do with the fight stopping. We might have reduced the damage done by the brawl but we hadn't stopped it. Those men had fought according to the natural surge and wane of adrenalin. We had stood back to back, side by side and supported each other. We didn't talk to each other and I needed no instruction. We had been a team.

Chapter 18
BARRY

WITHOUT WARNING, AND TO EVERYONE'S SURPRISE, THE ROYAL WAS SOLD. THE owner spent a Friday night running up and down the stairs between his office and his car with armfuls of booze and years of paperwork. And that was it. He was gone. The pub became the property of one of the corporate breweries. The staff quickly changed. The gays went first. They left in willy-willies of drama to be replaced by solid young men working towards corporate careers. A management structure was introduced and security was outsourced to Barry.

Barry owned All Australian Security. I had heard about him. No one could call himself a bouncer without having heard a story or two about Barry.

'Mate, this guy, don't get me wrong, this guy is hard,' Anefterios had told me. 'About as hard as things get these days. My brother worked for him years ago. Before they regulated the industry. I was just a tacker, mate, eighteen or something. But my bro, he was nineteen and training for a national title. Barry took him onto his crew. Ten or twelve guys, unlisted, unnamed, no numbers. Mate, these are fuckin' vigilantes. They'd smack cunts just for walking sideways. And some of these cunts were big, mate, and hard. None of this kung fu crap, these guys used to bite cunts' ears and noses off when things got going proper.'

'Bullshit.'

'I shit you not, one time one of these wrestler guys got a bloke called Blue to the ground, and goes for some choke hold, and Blue's face is a little close. Next thing Blue's just bitten through the cunt's ear!'

'Right. Is Blue, Barry?'

Please God. No.

'Fuck, no. Dunno what happened to Blue. Think he's in a prison in Thailand or something. Don't worry about it, grasshopper. There's a big difference between bouncers and the guys that manage them. Especially then. These guys were scared of no cunt and you've got a fuckin' dozen of 'em. Takes something special to manage that, and not just bein' extra crazy. Takes some brains, an edge.

'Gotta keep on top of the money an' the jobs. Crazy cunts like Blue and that, they get bored quick. They're not disciplined like boxers and cunts that train. They're just hard and loose and nasty. Don't keep 'em tethered mate, they'll just fly off the handle or off the face of the earth. They aren't guys interested in holding down a job. They do bouncing 'cos they get paid for bashin' cunts. You'da shit yourself if you ever saw one of these cunts.

'Anyway, Barry's older, right. He's been around for years. He's not scared of no one. He knows the guys he ought to be scared of, and he's still not fuckin' scared of 'em. One time – and I was there for this – we were outside a place where Barry's crew was working. My brother was working and I was just hanging around like a dumb cunt. Barry was there, half working and half mindin' his interests. You know those hot-dog stands that guys have outside pubs and clubs? Well, Barry had a bunch of guys doin' this for him, poor cunts who owed 'im money or something and they'd end up servin' hot dogs to pissed cunts till dawn. If they were a dollar short Barry'd cave their head in. Talk about a rock and a hard place!

'Anyway all of sudden this fella rolls up with his hot dog-trolley and parks a few yards down from Barry's guy. We were watching this and laughin' and thinkin', "Poor cunt". 'Cos we knew Barry was in the shop. We were dumb cunts like I said, and thought this cunt was just some dope givin' it a shot in the name of peace and justice. Barry but, he comes out, walks up to the guy real casual, has a chat, stands with the guy for a bit and then walks away. Comes and stands with my brother and me and some other cunt that's working and we ask, "What's goin' on?" 'Cos obviously we thought we'da seen something by then.

'And Barry explains to us that the guy's working for this mafioso, you know, the one that got topped the other year on the beach, him, but we didn't know this then. Barry says he's happy to wait and talk to Luigi or whatever the cunt's name was and go straight to the source of the rot, you know.

'So we wait there for a while, maybe two hours, cunts are getting thrown out and bashed around us the whole time. Barry never gets distracted. Couple of guys wrestled past 'im and he clocked 'em for fun but he was like a fuckin' game cat, mate, just waitin'. Finally the mob guy pulls up outside the club in a shiny black car, electric windows, driver, girls in the back, just like in a movie, just like he liked it, I reckon.

'Barry lets him pull up and start talking to the interloping hot-dog cunt and when the conversation is in flow, Barry just walks over in his suit, says hello to Luigi, opens the door and slams him in the chops.

Hard. Drags him out of the car, bitches in the car are screaming probably got coke and champagne spillin' down their thighs and Barry's holdin' their pimp against the car, breakin' ribs.

'Then he drags him over to the hot-dog stand and pulls the lid off a the boiler and just drives this cunt's face and head in and fuckin' holds it there. I don't know how fuckin' hot it was but I never heard anything like the screams that cunt made when Barry let him out. And, you know, with all the lights out the front of the club, man, he was lit up like something fuckin' big and bright. Barry just spat on him and called him cunt and walked off.'

I was silent for a time.

'How does he treat his employees?'

'Real good, s'long as you don't fuck up. He used to have this trick, right, if you can call it that. He figured that most places his lads worked were gonna get trouble, and that if they didn't get trouble then they didn't need bouncers. He needed places to need bouncers so he needed them to have trouble. If he showed up to a place where his guys were working anytime after 'bout eleven, he'd walk in and say, "Any trouble yet?" and if they say no he'd just walk up to the biggest, hardest-looking guy in the place and just fuckin' whack him, mate, and keep goin' till he had a good old brawl goin'.

'He fuckin' loved that shit. One time, I saw a guy hit him square in the face and Barry's just looked at the cunt and smiled and said, "Do that again, mate, come on give it to me." So, the guy hits him again harder, hard as he can, and Barry just wears it, mate. I swear the cunt just liked getting hit and then in one punch, he just fuckin' creamed this cunt. Guy was out for ten minutes. Pubs kept needin' bouncers.'

'How did he get away with that?'

'Grasshopper, there were no laws about it then. Being a bouncer didn't legally exist as a job. There were no duty of care issues. He might as well have been some cunt startin' a fight, which he was, and how was he gonna be traced? He was long gone by the time any cops showed, and if it was a bad one, so were his boys.'

'Is that how all the bouncing was done?'

'Anywhere that really needed it ended up with a crew like that.'

'Sounds like a self-fulfilling prophecy.'

'Eh?'

'Nothing. Was he just a street fighter?'

'Nah, mate. He was a boxer. Good one. Did it for too long. You'll see if you meet him, but, mate, he was a contender. Made a good livin' for a while and travelled the world, fightin' for money. He was born to it. Probably punched a hole in his mum's clacker to get out.'

So now Barry was my boss. All the guys working at the Royal went to meet Barry one morning at his offices. Alby, Anefterios, Ben and me.

Barry's office was tiny. He was, of course, huge. We squeezed ourselves in. Six men in a small room with a desk, one chair, a computer and a phone.

'Come in, fellas. Any of you guys know how to work a Motorola t50? Some arsehole gave it to me last night. Said it has a hundred bucks credit on it but I can't get the blasted thing to come on. Fuckin' toerag.'

'Pity that cunt.'

'Terry, I will ask you to keep a handle on that potty mouth of yours. This is a professional establishment and we have standards to uphold. If you and these gentlemen are to be in my employ, let us get started on the right foot. Gentlemen, you are?'

'Alby.'

'Ben.'

'Heath.'

'And Terry I know. Well, let's get started. Sorry about the office. Bit small, but we make do. New premises shortly.'

Barry's face was soft and swollen. His suit was well cut. He leant back easily in his chair and eyed the phone more carefully than us. His hair was cut formally but carelessly combed. Scar tissue sat round his eyes. The knuckle of his right middle finger was missing, sunken somewhere into the flesh of his hand. He looked us up and down. One eye wandered away from the other and away from us. The wandering pupil was smoky and far away, like a little daydream in a big, hard head.

'Well gentlemen, let me set this thing on its keel. I know what you boys get paid, and to be honest with you – which is what I aim to do and I expect the same of you and yours – you are getting more than my boys. This contract from the brewery, your pub is not the only one they've bought. I imagine you know this. Lucky bastard that I am, I scored the contracts for the bloody lot. Now, it's a sweet piece of pie, but not that sweet. I don't intend to give the bulk of my guys a rise any time soon, and you lot don't appear to me so invaluable as to be paid more than anyone else working for me …'

'Barry–'

'Shut up, Terry. I'll ask you to let me finish. To be honest with you all, if you were not already employed by the place, incumbent as it were,

I wouldn't hire you. You're too old. You two are too small and … Terry, well, I'd have to hire him. He's sort of family.'

'Now, look, the blokes I hire are big, young and tough as nails. I had a bloke get his abdominal wall severed with a pot glass last night and after beating the shit out of the toerag that done him, he bandaged hisself up and finished the shift. This fella's eighteen. Now I can see by the look of you lot that not one of you has that type of mettle. That's alright. That's not something to be ashamed of. Not everyone is cut out for the sort of expectations this firm makes of people. And for those people there are other firms and taxis to drive or whatnot. I am, however, in the business of earning a living, as are we all, and I am not one to bite the hand that feeds me.'

'You have been, mate.'

'As I said, Terry, I will ask you to refrain from speaking. Thank you, son.'

He called Terry 'son', and told him to shut up. I was no longer breathing.

'So, not being a fool I am obliged to consider the wishes of those providing me with the contracts for these many and various establishments. Which in this instance are as follows. They feel that they appeal to a particular clientele, a niche market, which you gentlemen are particularly gifted at managing and as such have requested that you remain in situ as a team with minimal inter-ference from my good self. They are prepared to pay the extra premium to allow me to make what I need and to pay you what you are accustomed to and as long as you can agree to some very simple terms, this is a workable proposition by my assessment. The terms I put to you are this. You will continue to be paid as you are now if you do not at any time expect to be treated as an employee of my company.

'All of you will agree not to discuss the amount you are paid, though the difference is a matter of two or three dollars per hour, with anyone outside of yourselves because we all know how such tidbits of information have a way of getting about on their own. You will manage yourselves and only Alby or Terry will need to contact me directly if you need extra staff. Am I making myself reasonably clear?'

'Crystal,' we chimed.

'If some other bloke from here comes to work with us, will you be paying him the extra just when he's at our place?'

'Besides the notion of precedence, Terry, what the bloody hell do you think I have been saying?'

'No.'

'Quite right. Now, Elaine at the front counter – I guess you already saw her – she has some contracts to sign. Thanks for dropping by gentlemen. I will endeavour to visit you at your place of work when I can. Goodbye.'

We signed our contracts and left. Outside, in the sunlight, we looked at each other. Terry had stayed inside.

'He never said his name, did he? Did you notice that?'

'Guess maybe we're s'posed to know that already.'

'Novel way to approach new employees.'

'It's pretty clear he sees us more as warts than employees. You alright with all this, Alby?'

'Fine. Less he bothers us the better.'

'Did you have anything to do with the stuff about niche markets and particular clienteles?'

'I had a word in Mark's ear before he left. Protected our interests.'

'Nice one.'

'Yeah, thanks. Doesn't hurt. Let's get out of here before he changes his mind,' said Ben.

Chapter 19

QUITTING OR 'THE B GENE'

After the sale, things changed. Ben moved to another state. Terry started to do a few extra shifts. Alby and I remained the core team, and we watched the culture of the staff change around us.

Barmen were hired and fired or lost and replaced on a weekly basis. No one except 'on shift' bar staff were allowed behind the bar or in the fridges. Managers watched the staff more as suspects than friends or possible bedmates.

Barry's summary judgement of us as sub-par bouncers had bothered me. Terry had told me over and over that size doesn't matter but now I knew that I lacked something that Barry could recognise in people. I was a bouncer, but I was never going to be the sort Barry wanted. It was September. Christmas was around the corner and without thinking too much about it, I told Alby I wanted to quit.

'What?'

'I'm gonna quit.'

'Why? I've told you, you'll miss it.'

'I know you have but, well, I'm still gonna quit.'

'What are you going to do?'

'Don't know.'

'You got work somewhere else? You can tell me.'

'No. I just, well, with Barry, I'm the little guy and I'm not crazy about being the little guy, I guess. Barry or guys like him might think I'm a joke but I don't feel like I'm growing anymore, and now …

'Not growing. That's a first, I reckon. No one's ever given that as a reason. Mate, don't quit just 'cos you think other guys don't think you can do it. Remember, they were all young once and smaller, and don't forget that they do this shit as a career. *A career!* You're doing other things with your life. This is the perfect part-time job. Do your training during the day. Your art. Then you come to work. Perfect. They give you a feed and you sit on your arse all night drinking peppermint tea.'

'I'm not saying I don't like it, but I'm not doing other stuff. I haven't even looked at a sculpture for more than a year.'

'Look, you're talking shit. It's a job. A j-o-b. Don't forget that. Think about it until next week and tell me then if you've made up your mind.'

'OK.'

A week later, I quit.

Being the person between people's daily self and their drunken, hair down, scream-when-you-laugh inner self meant having authority. It meant being able to say no to someone, and being supported by workmates. Bouncers are part of a modern-day guild, urban samurai that come out at night wearing black. We are the middlemen between chaos and order. There's something exciting and perverse about the position, and all you have to do is stand there with a number on your chest.

Bouncers talk of being hooked on the job. It's true.

The grumpy old bastard was right. I missed the job as soon as it was gone.

On my first weekend in three years that I wasn't standing at the door of the pub not one friend rang me. I had no idea what any of them were doing or if there were any parties on. I called a few mates but they were all busy. 'You're not working?' they all asked.

So that Friday night was spent in my room doing push-ups, lifting weights and trying to read a book. I hadn't read anything beyond martial arts magazines for eighteen months. I was struggling to decipher words with more than three syllables. I drank a few beers and kicked my punching bag for a half an hour. Walked the dog around a few blocks.

Training on Saturday was peculiar. I was so accustomed to being there without enough sleep that without realising it, I steamrolled an unsuspecting and very hung-over Lee before class, ran the class when it started and stayed training in the park an hour after everyone had left.

By nine o'clock Saturday night I was beside myself. I caught a tram into town. I went into a few bars and had a drink, but it's not the same being by yourself in a bar when you don't have a number on your chest. Your licence to look at people is revoked. I found myself visually reprimanded before I ended up at the Royal, standing next to Alby, feeling at home once more.

'Ahh … told yah you'd miss it, mate.'

'Mmm.'

'Didn't I, eh, didn't I tell you? What are you doing for work?'

'Nothing. Put my name down with some emergency teaching agencies. That should pick up pretty soon.'

'You want your job back, don't you?'

'Wouldn't say no.'

'But *I* have to. Barry already replaced you, and with that special deal on our pay, you'd have to get a job with him directly to be reinstated.'

'And we know what my chances of that are …'

The man in a bar who's been a bouncer is unmistakable. He's more erect and alert. He doesn't participate with the same abandon as others. His eyes constantly shift between his companion, the bar and the door. He becomes visibly attentive at loud or unusual noises. He never stands in the middle of the room. The edgy guy in black is probably an off-duty bouncer. Old bouncers never die, they just stand in corners, watching.

Here I was. Twenty-eight and already in bouncer limbo. Not employed. Not wanted by my old employer and feeling that bouncing was the only skill I had. Sure I was a qualified teacher and a qualified artist – whatever the hell that meant – but my connection to reality, the thing that made me feel I had a place in the world, the role that had come to define me, was gone. I thought of Barry's scorn for us in his office.

'Fuck him,' I thought. 'I can do this shit. It's what I do.'

I called Lee. 'G'day mate … yeah good … no, still at a loose end … look mate, have you got that number you mentioned for the guy at that club you said was looking for security? … Yeah, thought I'd give it a shot.'

Chapter 20
JOHNNY TOO-COOL

'HELLO.'

'Ah, hello. John?'

'Johnny.'

'Right, Johnny. How are you? Heath. Sorry I'm a little early.'

'No problems.'

It was five in the afternoon. The lane was innocuous but dirty. Round the door was litter of cigarette butts and straws. Johnny was a fair-haired man of maybe thirty, with almond-shaped eyes and contrived stubble. Good-looking in a half-hearted way. I was meeting to discuss my trial appointment to the security staff. He said, 'You been here before?'

'Yeah, couple of months ago.'

'How was it?'

'Good. Pretty busy. Plenty of people.'

'Right, but how was the vibe?'

'Um, good. Seemed pretty good.'

'You know, people coming and going?'

'It was busy, is that what you mean?

'Mmm. Were they beautiful?'

'Beautiful? Some of them were. Yeah, some were definitely beautiful.'

'More beautiful people than other places you've worked?'

'Well, younger, and, yeah, I guess more beautiful, but you know, I haven't ...'

'That's what I mean ... we have more beautiful people, more people that are on the edge, making more waves than anywhere else. That's our vibe. Young, beautiful, intelligent and drinking cocktails.'

'Niche market.'

'Totally. We are accessing a market that has never been seen before in Melbourne. We are creating a previously non-existent clientele.'

'Really?'

'People that didn't used to go out at night, who couldn't be bothered with the humdrum of the entertainment status quo, are coming out now, out of the woodwork down from their warehouses to sit in our club, to drink our cocktails, and look at each other and see that there are other people out there like them.'

'Yeah, right. I'm pretty keen to work here. Young staff, new venue.'

'You've nailed it. This is the new breed of venue and we are looking for a new breed of security. That's our thing, man. Creativity. We are looking at every angle to find ways of being creative, going in new directions. We want to walk where no club has walked before.'

'That's a big call.'

'Since we opened, three months ago, the face of Melbourne nightlife has changed. People hear about us, but they don't know where to find us. We don't advertise and our phone number is not listed.'

'And your front door is a fire door in a laneway off a laneway.'

'Totally. The harder we are to locate, in geographical terms, the bigger we are in cultural terms. That is the essence of cool and we have made it into a place.'

'Would you like me to come down when you're open, to see the place when it's going?'

'Yeah you can start on Friday. Three months' trial and then we re-assess. Sound OK? No need to come for a look, everyone wants to work here so come and work out when you are going to start with the guys on the door. Sound cool?'

'Sure. Thanks.'

'Ok, great. Bring your tax file number and bank details and pass them in to the manager. Great to meet you, man. I'm sure you'll fit into the vibe like hand and glove.'

I made my way out of the city with all the other people going home, savouring that narrow space between an old job and a new one, where everything is possible.

Chapter 21
CRACK TEAM

I TURNED RIGHT INTO A TINY NAMELESS LANE WHERE THE BIG BROWN FIRE ESCAPE door hung open. A picket fence ran three metres from the door to where a velvet rope swung between the last picket and a rendered brick wall. At the rope a rough queue of people fifteen deep waited. A single light globe lit the area and on the opposite side of the lane was a tired-looking Ford with hi-fi speakers on the roof playing a crackling broadcast of Triple R.

The only visible security was a man shorter than me, and slighter. He was wearing a necklace, had soft skin and beautiful eyes. I shouldered my way through the small crowd until I was at the rope and face to face with the man. He said hello. I said hello, ducked under the rope and told him I was there to see Raffie.

He looked at me, stunned.

'I'm going to be working here,' I said.

'Well that explains it. What's your name?'

'Heath.'

'Yeah, yeah, right. Now I remember. Fuck, sorry, man. Stupid of me. I should have known when you just came under the rope like that. I'm Charles and that's Lou.' Lou was the girl who handled the money. She stood just beyond the rope, in between Charles and her post at the door.

He turned to the queue waiting at the rope like earnest children at a quiet crossing.

'Sorry guys. Members only tonight. Won't be able to help any of you.'

A gentleman in head-to-toe designer wear began speaking to us. Charles interrupted him, 'Not any of you, mate. Cheers. See ya.'

Most of the small crowd filed away down the lane to our left. Charles faced me, turning his back on the snubbed man. I wouldn't show my back to a patron, even with a rope between us. Charles was not a bouncer like Anefterios or Alby. I was blinded by the chutzpah. He strutted behind the rope, that symbolic division between club and public with all the confidence and bravado of the biggest, most experienced bouncers. He was a door bitch. Most male door-bitches are mincy, effeminate men, and more often than not gay. Charles wasn't mincy and I guessed not gay, but he was not a bouncer. I looked closer.

'What you'll be doing down here is backing me up. We've had trouble finding people to work here who aren't really aggressive, you know, looking for fights. Anyway, I do the door, the talking, I mean. I select the customers. What we need you to do is just be there to kind of add weight …'

I wasn't sure he was looking at the right guy. Size isn't everything, but it's something.

'OK. Who else is there?'

'Raffie on Fridays and Johnny on Saturdays. His gaze shifted. 'Guys, can't help you tonight. SEE YA!'

The last stragglers left, deflated.

'Has Raffie done security before?'

'No. He's pretty fit, though. I mean, he smokes a pack or two a day, but he does a lot of running.'

'Right. The club been open long?'

'Since last August, except for a month over Christmas.'

I wanted to ask questions, starting with, 'Are you crazy?' But I also wanted the job.

'So what shifts will I be doing?'

'Thursday from ten till close, about three-thirty. Friday and Saturday from eleven till five-thirty.'

A young couple came to the rope. I retreated so Charles could tell them we were full. Without looking away from me, he reached out, unhooked the rope and let them in, saying, 'Five dollars cover tonight, guys.'

The couple were no different from those he'd turned away a minute before.

'What nights are you … we open?'

'Tuesday, Wednesday, Thursday, Friday, Saturday and Sunday. Yeah.'

He turned from me.

'Hi guys, come on in. Yeah. Five dollars cover. Nice shirt, buddy.'

He turned back to me, 'The nights you work it'll be me, you and an owner downstairs and Philip upstairs. If it works out, you'll probably get to do the door some Saturdays and I'll get the night off.'

'Sure.'

This bouncing game was a lark or a cash cow for Charles. A Saturday night off from one venue was a Saturday night to spend in another venue. Not a night off. Friday and Saturday nights were a bouncer's working week.

What this guy was doing had nothing to do with bouncing. He was too buoyant, he retained a faith in humanity.

'Does it get busy?'

'Capacity of two-seventy. Down here it can get pretty crazy. We had a queue from here to half way up the lane just before you got here. It'll pick up again. Always does. We keep a track of the numbers with an 'In' clicker and 'Out' clicker.'

I'd noticed him clicking them when people came in.

Cheering broke out in the stairwell. Women's shoes click clacked. Squeals and laughter grew. I looked towards the foot of the stairs. Stocking and denim-clad legs cascaded into view. Revellers spilled out, but before leaving they kissed Charles. The rope's unhooked end swayed foppishly in his hand as he hugged and kissed.

'See you, baby. Yeah, yeah, for sure. Bye bye. No, you call me. NO. You CALL ME. OK, OK, OK, I'll call. Yeah, good luck with it, man. Love to Sue. Yeah, tell her she rocks. Whoo, hey, don't touch my arse when I'm working. Did you bring me a drink? BITCH! Have fun guys, yeah, yeah, yeah. Love you, too. See ya. Bye.'

It was a virtuoso performance. I was enchanted. He looked into the eyes of everyone as they left and he gave them all some love, something to take home. He might not have been a bouncer but I could learn a lot from him.

A man who had left with the group stopped just outside the fence, in front of Charles and me. He stood with his weight on his left leg. His left hand waved high and lazy in melodramatic arcs. He wore grey suit pants and a pair of Birkenstock sandals. His shirt was stuck to his back with sweat, the original cerulean blue now a seeping cyan that steamed in the cool night. His hair, too, was wet. He turned slowly to us, letting his raised arm swing down to his hip and take his upper body through an exhausted ripple that said he had just completed a chapter of his evensong.

'Man, those kids are crazy, you know. Like they're so crazy. Man. It's wild, they just love the place. They come every week, every week, no matter what. I really reckon they should all come in free, Charles, they're just so good for the place. Their energy is just sooo GOOD, God.'

This guy was wearing a security number too. His pants were so low that curling wet sprigs of pubic hair sprouted from the waistline. He smiled a lopsided grin at us.

Charles said, 'Philip, this is Heath. He's going to do Thursdays, Fridays and Saturdays.'

'Cool. Yeah, hey, man, how are you?'

Philip shook my hand, propped his elbow on the fence and lit a cigarette.

'Yeah, you'll love the place. Yeah, you will. It'll be great. Oh, it's just GREAT up there tonight. Fuck, Charles, you're doing a great job tonight. Geez, it's fuckin' cold down here. I'm going back upstairs. Come up in a minute and I'll show you around, dude. Fuck, I gotta get back up there.'

He idled on up the stairs with a parting joke for Lou, or Louise, who ran down to Charles and me. She barrelled into Charles, but as he put his arms around her she pushed him strongly away. It appeared that they were lovers. She exclaimed, 'He's off his fuckin' tree! Did you guys see that? My god. It's not even two-thirty.'

'It is, babe … nearly.'

'No way!'

She overflowed with laughter.

'He's off his chops. He'll be up there dancing his arse off.'

'Ssssh.' Charles warned her, because I was there, I guessed.

I agreed with her. Philip's eyes had looked like fried eggs. Charles ushered Louise back to her post at the money desk at the foot of the stairs and greeted four patrons.

'Hey, guys. How are you tonight?

'Good. Yeah. Cheers. Good, thanks.' They chorused.

Charles lowered the rope and in they filed. No sooner had the rope been replaced on its pole than Charles was saying to a group of three men with matching haircuts, shirts three shades of pale and distressed denim, 'Sorry, guys, guest list only tonight. Members and guestlist. Can't help you.'

'Yeah, mate, we're on Chris Skelly's list from Bite Media.'

Charles glanced at the pin board for less than a second.

'Sorry, guys. Not there. Can't help. Members and guests only. See ya.'

Again he turned his back on a group of unknown men.

'Come on mate, we just want to go up for a drink. It's our mate's birthday. We won't even be there more than half an hour. We don't mind paying the door charge. Come on, mate.'

Charles turned around. Looked them up and down, making no attempt to hide his assessment of them.

'Like I said, guys. Can't let you in unless you're on the guest list or have members' passes. Have a good night.'

The three men waited a few moments and wandered away up the laneway.

'What do members' passes look like?' I asked.

'Don't exist yet.'

'Shall I take that as my first important lesson?'

'You should. I'll call Philip down and we can go up and I'll show you the place.'

Charles walked to the door. Just inside was a small telephone, an intercom. He held the receiver to his ear, pressed a button and waited.

'Hey, there, it's Charles … Yeah! … How are you two? … Yeah … Can you find Philip and send him down? … Great. Thanks …'

He hung up. 'He'll be down in a sec and we can go up.'

Philip took fifteen minutes to come rolling down the stairs holding two bottles of water, one that he handed to Louise. Philip was struggling to stand straight. He shouted, 'Go for it, guys. Man, I need a rest. Fuck, it's just crazy up there. It's just going off.'

The staircase climbed on for another three flights, with large landings between them. Each flight was ceilinged by the next level of stairs. The walls were painted white and the stairs brown. It was claustrophobic. The first floor fire door was the entrance to the club. Just inside, next to a glowing cigarette dispenser and a closed blue door I asked, 'Is that the only way to communicate between upstairs and downstairs?'

'Yeah … this is the office. You won't need to go in here, not for a while anyway.'

I wanted to return to the topic of the door but the tour had begun.

'The guys have tried to create a space which is not obviously a chill-out space, more like a separate space between the bar and entrance. We call it the hunting lounge ...'

The hall opened into a room with green felt tiles for flooring. A glass-topped wicker table and matching chairs were clustered to my right. A gaudy coloured glass chandelier the size of a watermelon sprayed yellow green and orange dots on the people seated there. On the left of this couch were two replica carriage lights complete with flame-shaped orange globes flickering. These lit the floor in front of double glass doors that swung back and forth constantly as people came and went. Beyond these, double glass doors swung back and forth constantly as people came and went.

'The space is more fluid when we prop the doors open, you know, people come and go more easily and there's less sense of a shift between spaces but the music can be heard from the bar, which really changes this area.'

To our left was a U-shaped seating area. This one was a lot bigger, with twenty or more people seated on its pony-hide cushions. The wall at its back was covered in spiralling seventies tiles lit strongly and in crisp yellow and green glazed patterns. Patrons were laughing and squirming together in orgiastic conversation silhouetted by the tiles. The music was the chanting of a Navajo Indian chief. (I know because I checked the CD cover later.) We were standing now in the middle of the space. A wood, leather and ceramic light fixture was directly above my head. I craned my neck to see it more clearly.

'Wild isn't it? When people are really pissed you can suggest that they come out here for a bit instead of having to leave.'

I tried to imagine Anefterios suggesting someone could sit for some fresh air, to get themselves together. It didn't come easily to mind.

'I'll show you the toilets.'

There were chest-high shelves outside each toilet. On the left shelf was a kitsch plaster Pomeranian with a ribbon in its hair, and on the right a plaster Pug in a bowler hat.

The men's toilet had a tiled beige floor which extended up the walls to knee height. The walls were covered in a cheap wood laminate and dark brown edges divided them into rectilinear segments. Each segment had been covered in clear perspex. Were it not for three men with their dicks in their hands it might have been an alpine spa room.

The women's toilet was different.

'The guys toilet is really like, trying to make the most of a small space, hence the kind of sauna look they went for, yeah? But with the women's … hey baby, what's up?'

A woman had stepped out of the toilet, tits super bra-ed and sparkly. She cupped Charles's nuts and planted him a long tongue kiss before sliding away back to the dance floor.

'Where was I, yeah, they wanted a more social space, a meeting place, a little more intimate than the hunting lounge.'

'Do you know her well?'

'Who?'

'That girl who just bit a chunk off your face?'

'Pretty wild, eh? The toilets are along the back wall, but down the end there's the little couch and the sink has been built into this bench.'

The brown and orange fibreglass sink ran the length of the left wall and was lit with tiny overhead spots. Ladies checked their lips and boobs, washed their hands and blew joints around us, paying no attention to the number Charles was wearing. On the small couch at the end of the room, a young woman sat astride a man with her skirt up and the two of them, while grinding against each other, were holding a conversation with an emaciated-looking man next to them. It was sort of like being inside a late sixties record cover, all ochre tones and flesh.

'Check this out. Sorry, love.'

Charles grabbed my arm and we pushed in front of a woman to take our place in the cubicle that had just been vacated. Charles was a new kind of bouncer to me. I wondered if he had gone to bouncer college and if it had been anything like my experience.

'Check it out.'

The cubicle space doubled the men's. Behind the cistern, at chest height was a shelf. It was brown, as was the paint on the walls. In the middle of the shelf was a thirty-by-ten centimetre rectangle of under-lit white perspex. The tour continued.

'So the guys are kind of saying, well, we know what people go out for. They want a place that is basically their living room with better decor. They want to feel free, like the Primal Scream track, you know. People take drugs, we accept that and we just try and keep them safe. People drink and get messy, but why would we throw them out when they're drunk? They've spent a lot of money in the place and we owe them a duty of care.'

'Duty of care? It's illegal to have intoxicated people on the premises.'

'Yeah, but that's the letter of the law. We both know it's a fucking sham. If someone is blind but holding a decent conversation and paying for drinks, you leave 'em alone. It's not about intoxication, it's about behaviour. We're trying to come at that from a more sort of pastoral angle, yeah?'

'Pastoral?'

'Totally. Look at the relationship between the customers and security. Wait till you see Philip on the floor, man. He's the centre of people's experience, which gives him plenty of leverage when he needs it.'

It was a beautiful and hopeful thing to think that this job could be done without paranoia and suspicion. I was in no hurry to challenge the fantasy. I came out of the pastoral Shangri-la Charles had painted just enough to point out that we were still standing in a woman's toilet cubicle.

'Ssshhh, listen.' He whispered.

A man's voice came from the cubicle on our left. It was Philip.

'On Thursday, it was really good, I mean Friday, yeah yesterday, no Thursday, fuck – yesterday was great, but the music just had a bit more of an edge to it …'

'Yeah, yeah.' A woman replied.

'It was a bit sharper. Tonight it's just sort of rosy.'

'Totally.'

'It just carries you.'

'Totally.'

Charles looked impishly at me, a grin splitting his face.

He signalled for me to climb onto the toilet seat with him. The woman's voice was excited.

'Can you really get me a membership?'

'Of course, of course, what are we snorting?'

'Just a pill.'

'Ooh a dove, fun fun fun.'

We peered over the wall of the cubicle. On the perspex window of white light Philip was sliding a credit card through a pile of pink powder, arranging it into two long lines. The girl was rolling a ten-dollar note into a tube. I understood the lit shelf.

The woman chose and snorted her line first, her head bending over the shelf, the rolled note in one hand and hair held back with the other. We heard the whispery sound as she sucked it in, then she tilted her head back to encourage the powder into her sinuses. Charles didn't flinch, and signalled for the girl to say nothing. She smiled complicitly. Philip lowered his head to the drugs, and Charles bellowed, 'PHILIP!'

In mid-snort Philip's lungs changed direction and pink powder was blown in a spreading cloud off the light, against the walls and onto the floor. His body went rigid and he lost his footing. His hand instinctively grasped for support but slipped on the edge of the toilet seat and slid into the S-pipe with a gentle plop. On his knees, he held his face and swore. He stood, turned around and looked up. Pink pill powder smeared savagely across his cheeks and his elbow was dripping with cistern water. Charles was howling with laughter.

'Fuckin' hell, man.'

Philip's eyes were a terrible red and his hair stood out from his head in shock. He toyed with the bridge of his nose, sniffling and inhaling to catch the last of the powder as it dribbled out.

'I fuckin' shat myself Charles. Fuck. What a fuckin' waste. Charles, apologise to Naomi.'

Philip started muttering to himself and absent-mindedly drying his arm on Naomi's jacket. She looked in horror and retreated from the cubicle.

Charles and I left the cubicle and the toilet.

'Shall we continue the tour?'

'Sure. That wasn't particularly pastoral …'

'No, s'pose not. Funny, though.'

The double glass doors opened onto the dance floor and a wall of sound. The subsonic boom of the bass pulsed around us. Charles looked at me with glee.

'Wwooooooooohhooooooooo. I just fuckin' love that. I never get sick of it, never!' he screamed, as we were swamped by noise. The house music was a seductive mix of throbbing bass and electronic melody.

The beat drove more than just dance. The selling of secrets and the clapping of hands, the running of sweat and the touching of skin, the making of friends, the forging of love. People were bathing in sex, love and dance.

The bar was crowded five people deep.

'The music's not so loud here. There's only these four speakers. When we get up towards the dance floor you might have trouble hearing me.'

Behind the bar, impeccably dressed men and women prepared drinks in a blur of can-tops popping, the wet strum of cocktail shakers and the 'phhht' of European beer caps being wrested from their bottle. These guys were in a different class to those at the Royal. They were professionals.

The bottles were stored on a pyramid of glass shelves supported by ornate pillars of coiling, blue-and-gold painted plaster. Light bounced off curtains of threaded circular mirrors (which hid tall, green rubbish bins) and reflected onto the tower of bottles.

Banks of clear vodka bottles and dark brown scotch, white rum and gin were at the first level of the bar with the silver ranks of shakers. There were tall glasses full of long spoons and whisks, wooden muddlers and lovely low, white bowls of salt, sugar and cinnamon.

The higher shelves held the lollipop colours of cocktail mixers, the sick yellows and greens of Strega, Chartreuse and Midori, the subtler browns of single malts, the rich ochre of Hennessy and the ominous amber of four different Tequilas. On the highest shelf, beyond the reach of most, was Absinthe, glimmering green and friendly.

'Is this busy for the bar?'

'Pretty busy. Gets worse but this is pretty full on. Come on, let's get through it. Check out the couches along that wall, there'll be heaps of trashbags, the ones who'd like to be up the front but can't move that far.'

Behind the queue for the bar against the wall were square couches in the house materials of vinyl and hide. Strewn over them like forgotten scarves were people who would have been thrown out hours before by any bouncer I had worked with.

From a big black box at the end of these couches a low, peninsula of sound was reaching out into the dance floor. Charles's lips were moving but the sound swallowed every word.

I followed him through the throng. People were sweating and wet, eyes closed or rolling back in their head. Arms were in the air and pelvises rolled and bolted at each other. The dancing was unashamedly suggestive.

We stepped up a level to the highest point in the club, a carpeted area behind the DJ. There a woman bounced gently, pigtails brushing her headphones and a cigarette stuck to her lip. It was quieter up here. I could see over the heads of the dancers and the people queuing at the bar all the way back to the double glass doors. It was a mass of dancing, drinking, ecstatic clubbers.

Behind us were more couches smeared with prone bodies, some writhing, some sleeping.

Floor to ceiling windows had been cut into the front of the building.

'Nice view, huh?'

'Beautiful.'

'Nah dude, the dance floor,' Charles corrected. 'From here you can see the whole place. When people are dancing the place really works, you know, 'cos it's so long and thin. If people are just hanging around at the bar, the dance floor is like this canyon of stale space and there is all this congestion around the bar. People come in from the street and can't get through. It's just not what they need to see. This is where I come to get a view of the night, to try and understand how I'm doing on the door. This is where it's all reflected for me.'

Yeah?'

'Sure.'

'Let's get back to the door. Don't want to leave Philip down there too long. You gonna stay up here or come down?'

'I'll come down.'

We made our way back through the club. I just followed Charles. Did I want to work here? Could I be like these guys? Did I want to be? Were they naive and deluded or were they visionaries? What was all that talk about the space? It sounded like drivel, but I was somehow inspired by it.

We wound our way back through the dancers, along the bar and through the corridor. The lounge was refreshingly cool and quiet after the bar and dance floor. Down the brown fire escape stairs, past Louise who pounced on Charles for a kiss, and out to the picket fence. Philip was smoking and talking with a man in a puffy down jacket.

'Totally. Yeah man, fuck, absolutely. Look, man, it's been really good talking. I'll pass your disc onto Jools, and yeah, Tuesday night, man, come down. We can chat more. I'm here from ten, and yeah, we'll work it out. See ya later, thanks bro.'

The guy wandered off down the dark lane. Philip turned his fried egg eyes to us.

'Fuck, guys. Crazy music on the R's. A minute ago, Iggy was on and now you can hear it. Just mad, they've gone, forget the parameters, forget the categories we're just gonna go all out and play stuff that, that ...'

He gyrated his hips for effect, flicked his half-smoked fag high into the air, pointed to the sky, blew out smoke in a hard grey line and bounded up the stairs.

I was ready to go home. 'I'm gonna head off, guys.'

Charles started. 'Oh, shit. You haven't met Raffie yet.'

'If you want me to come in next Thursday and Friday I can meet him then.' I didn't want to go back upstairs.

'Come in for sure, man. Fuck, I thought I made that clear. You'll be great. Start next Friday, say round nine. Anything you want to ask me?'

'What do I need to bring to get through the night?'

'Clothes and food.'

'And where did Philip work before? How long has he been doing this?'

'He was a boilermaker south of Perth somewhere.'

'Really?'

'Really, really. Beneath that dancing queen exterior is a man who can fix anything with a rubber band and a hairclip.'

'Righto.' What planet had I landed on? I smiled bleakly.

'What do you do, when you're not here?'

'Was and am an interior designer.'

Got it.

CHAPTER 22
TOP THREE

Saturday night. My third week at the club. Friday night had been busy and I'd spent a lot more time dealing directly with people at the rope. I was getting used to lying to people. Charles was patient with me. He never lost his cool and never succumbed to customer pressure. No was no, and if they wanted to wait an hour, they could.

I arrived at eleven. No one was at the rope. I let myself through and turned left behind the picket fence. Inside the door of the building Charles was cuddling with Louise.

'Evening folks.'

'Hey man, how are ya?'

'Good thanks, Lou, good evening.'

'Good evening.'

Charles squeezed my right bicep.

'Been training? You're looking pumped.'

'Yeah.'

He looked at Lou. 'This guy, just the gym, just the gym, like it's no big deal.'

It wasn't. A year and a half since first visiting Anefterios at his gym, my body had grown accustomed to weights. It still hurt when I changed routines, but going to the gym and wearing out my body on exercise that didn't require fine-motor coordination was a way to relax. It calmed my mind and quieted the fear that still ran through me before a night at work. I found comfort in the dull thud of soreness, the feeling three hours after a session when blood started to run free in my muscles again. It made me feel quiet to go to the gym and lift weights, to skip for half an hour afterwards, through the wall of exhaustion, until, birds flew inside me and I was free of the world, of judgement, of fear.

'I'll go sign on.'

'Sure, muscles,' said Charles and went back to teasing Louise.

There were hardly any people in the bar. Give or take a few shadowy corners. Caz, the stick-like manager, was on the customer side of the bar smoking a cigarette and complaining to Tim, the first barman in. He was chopping limes. I signed on, clipped number thirty-seven to my shirt, helped myself to a lemonade and went back around the bar to say hello to Bel, the manager.

'Hi, beautiful.' She slid off her stool and gave me an ambiguous kiss on the lips. She had a nose like a horse and her collarbones were bigger than her breasts. She was so white and her hair dyed so black, she could only be a nightclub manager.

'Hi. Good week?'

'Oh, you know, five nights here, you?'

'Trained, went to the gym, walked my dog.'

'Such a bouncer.'

'Yep that's me, born bouncer, in the blood.'

'You're full of shit, eh?' Caz said, touching my arm a little too long.

'Well, have a good night guys, see you at the other end.' I headed for the door.

'Unless we need you to save our arses,' Tim called out behind me.

Charles and Lou were arguing.

'No way Lou, there is no way I would ever have said that.'

'Charles, why would I make that up?'

'Sweetheart, I don't know, but you must have 'cos that is just about top three in my lamest scenes.'

'Bullshit.'

'What's up?'

'Well,' Charles explained, 'we were talking about our top three *Star Wars* scenes.'

'*Charles* was talking about his top three scenes,' said Lou.

'Like you don't have one?'

'I wouldn't if it wasn't in our top three post-coital topics.'

'Ignore her, she loves it.'

'What are your top three *Star Wars* scenes?' I asked.

'No way man, I tell you first you might steal one of mine. Tell me yours first.'

'I haven't really thought about it.'

'Well, you should.'

'No, he shouldn't, well-adjusted people don't spend their time thinking about these things,' interjected Lou.

'Come on, Heath, give us one quick one, trust-your-instincts and you can spend the rest of the night thinking of your other two.'

'I tell you one, you tell me one.'

'Deal.'

'Ten, nine, eight, seven, six …'

'Early in the first one, episode four, after the rebels have escaped or whatever and we meet Darth for the first time and he kills his commander without touching him.'

'Really?' Lou looked scared.

'I guess so,' I felt ugly and brutish.

'Don't listen to her, she's got the fucking ewoks in her top three.'

'I do not.'

'Bullshit. You do.'

'What's your number three?' I cut them off.

'Right, number three comin' up. "Red leader standing by red two, standing by just like beggars' canyon back home. Close your eyes Luke, let the force guide you, Ben." Rebel attack on the death star at the end of episode four, Ben Kenobi returns to Luke for the first time and Luke blows the shit out of the Death Star with a single shot. The good stealing a victory from the forces of evil. George Lucas, where did you go so wrong?'

'Episode one?'

'Episode fucking one. The anticlimax of so many young lives. How many people waited decades for that fart of a film. How could he get it so wrong?'

'Technology.'

'Eh?'

'Technology. The thing George thought the first three needed more of. He animated half the cast of the new ones just 'cos he could. In *Star Wars*, Chewy, C3PO, they're human. Even R2 had a dwarf in them.'

'Thought about this a bit have you?'

'A little.'

'And we thought you were just hired muscle. Surprising to hear a guy with a number on his chest and muscles analysing movies,' Lou said.

'What about me?' Charles exclaimed.

'Apart from you, baby.'

I felt warm inside. These people were becoming friends. With Lou and Charles and even Philip, I felt part of a team. The team had not been tested yet but morale was high and that counted for something.

'What's your number three, Lou?' I interrupted.

They stopped arguing. Charles went out to the rope to let some people in. I stood against the cold, old white painted brick wall next to Lou. The couple came to her pokey desk.

'Five bucks each, guys,' she said

'Already? Bit early isn't it?' the man of the pair said. Young, expensively dressed and tanned.

'From ten.'

'Shit,' turning to his dim-looking date he asked, 'Still wanna go in?'

'Yeah, baby. I've been looking forward to this all week.'

'OK.' He pulled out ten dollars and handed it to Lou.

'Thanks.'

With a grunt they were gone up the stairs.

'They are the future,' Charles said returning from the rope.

'What?'

'In six months or a year, that will be what just about everyone upstairs looks like,' Lou said grimacing.

'Why?'

'Because,' Charles explained, 'they represent the clubland mainstream. It is a sad fact that no club is exempt from it.'

'Isn't that what we're doing, not letting the mainstream, whatever that is, in?'

'Yeah, but we're fighting a losing battle. We can only hold out against a natural force for so long. The cool kids will move on, the la-di-da's that make Johnny so happy and in their place will be the wogs.'

'Why did you let them in then?' I asked.

'Nothing for it tonight. Have to.'

'Hey?'

'Eddie B is playing.'

'Right?'

'Eddie B. DJ'ing since he was sixteen. He's a legend. Anywhere he plays will have a full house. They just happen to not be our preferred client base. Most of them will be here to see Eddie B and won't even notice the place.'

'If they can find it,' Lou added.

'Why hire a DJ that will attract a large crowd that we don't really want?' I asked.

'Haven't spent long in the club scene have you, young Jedi?'

'No.'

'There are DJ's that every club wanting to get the right mentions in the street press invites for the owners to special gigs etc. They have to be put on the calendar from time to time. Besides, Melbourne's only got so many DJs and if clubs rotate their DJs like us, that means occasionally going outside your comfort zone.' Charles went back to the rope after he said this. Lou and I followed him.

'So we're talking about DJ diplomacy. Greasing the wheels?' I was enthralled.

'That's exactly it. Catches on quick for a bouncer, doesn't he, Lou?'

'Sure does. Eddie is a really, really good house DJ. He just happens to have this huge following of suburban wogs. I'm a wog too, so I know. They are a horde, but they love their music.'

'Do they drink?' It seemed a stupid question as I said it but so many people took ecstasy and drank nothing but water in the club.

'Yes and no,' said Charles.

'They either drink bourbon and coke all night or they get e'd off their face and just drink water,' Lou explained.

'Pray for the eckies. A group of twenty wogs on ecstasy is a much nicer thought than twenty wogs tanked to the eyeballs on Bourbon,' Charles said, looking at me firmly.

'Mmm. See your point.'

The night was cool. A mild breeze snaked its way down the laneway and was sucked in the door of the club. In the laneway we could see some stars in the horizontal sliver of sky above us and some small clouds wandered across our view like lost sheep. For twenty minutes we didn't get a chance to talk. A trickle of people came to the door, which Charles was supervising. I would have said no to all of them the week before, and Charles would have, too. Lou sat alone under cover at her desk and stool. I stood behind Charles and watched. He was a short man. This made me feel more like a bouncer. I was visually the biggest on the team. Size isn't everything, but when you're still pumped from a gym session and looking down the barrel of a Saturday night, it's a crutch.

Just before midnight the flow of people stemmed. Lou came down from her roost and Charles turned around to face the two of us.

'Gonna be busy,' he said. 'Feel it in my bones.'

A little after one am, out of sight, a bottle exploded under a car tyre at the top of the lane. The rumble of an engine came towards us and with the muffled blare of speakers leaking through closed windows, Philip rolled around the corner in his old Ford. Climbing across the bench seat, rolling out of the passenger door and lighting a cigarette, he stood and greeted us.

'My darlings!'

'Philip,' we chorused.

His trousers were the same as last night, but his shirt was different. Tonight it was a tight standard issue Mcdonald's shirt. His hair was lank and greasy, stuck behind his ears and parted in the middle. Dark rings around his eyes, red-rimmed eyelids and pupils that vibrated with amphetamines told us he hadn't slept.

'How was the rest of last night?' Charles asked.

'Great, man. Fucking rocked.'

'What time did you get out of there?'

'About five.'

'Gee that's alright, we only left here at three-thirty,' I said.

'Nah man, five pm. Love that fucking twenty-four hour licence,' Philip drawled, correcting me.

'Guys I'm just going to put some names on the door, they're great people, and they're just so excited about seeing Eddie B play tonight.'

'Free?' Lou asked.

'Yeah, yeah, won't be many of them,' Philip said. He wrote three names on the door list that hung on the inside of the picket fence.

'There we go, three names.' As he said this he added plus four next to each.

'How are all you guys? Oh excuse me.' He stepped aside for three young women who had come to the door from the left where we couldn't see them.

'Hi guys,' Charles greeted the girls.

'Five dollars tonight, just wait there a second folks, it's five dollars tonight guys, that's cool? Come on in.'

A small crowd had followed the girls without warning. As the six men entered it was obvious that they were all in the same party. Charles turned to me and whispered, 'Classic technique, send the hot chicks in the group ahead to get the doorman soft then follow with the main group immediately. On another night I would have stopped them.'

Music surrounded us as the voices of the patrons faded up the stairs. Philip had pulled out the old hi-fi speakers that were rigged up in his car and arranged them on the roof. An electronic, metronomic beat bounced back and forth between the walls and away up the lane.

'There we go folks, wired for sound.' Philip came inside the rope and was on his way upstairs when Lou asked, 'Phil, what's your number one *Star Wars* moment?'

He stopped. Looked at us. We all smiled at him as he began to nod his head, gently point his hand and cigarette at us and a big grin crept across his dishevelled face. When he smiled, even in his state, his face danced. He was charming.

'Nice one, nice one, nice one, yeah. Yeah, I like it, OK, OK. Let's see now. So many ways to go. Are we talking *Star Wars* episode four or all three of the first trilogy, or, tell me, are we including episode one?'

'You can include episode one but if your all-time favourite is in that … we have to kill you,' Charles said. Philip laughed, coughed, spat over the fence, dragged on his cigarette and looked at Charles.

'Too true. Tell you what. I'm gonna sign on and get a drink. Then I'll come down and tell you. Busy up there?'

'Getting there. Maybe one-fifty so far,' I said.

'Back in a minute.' He went up the stairs.

More people came down the lane. Young Italian men and women. Hair and breasts carefully arranged. Clothes impeccable and boring. Charles let them in. Last week, no way. More followed and soon there was a queue of thirty people. I stood silently behind Charles as he sorted the crowd. Men looked me up and down as they came in. They knew I was 'the bouncer' and they were assessing me. The crowd continued until the little clickers said two hundred people were upstairs. It was a monotonous parade tonight. I could see why the owners dreaded the 'mainstream'. This club aimed for an inner city clientele, people who designed clothes or bought expensive, individual garments. If enemy of cool is sameness; tonight's crowd was the Phantom Menace.

'I'm going to the toilet.' Lou called and disappeared upstairs.

I did the money while she was gone. It was moving into peak hour. Thirty came in while Lou was upstairs. People started leaving, asking for pass-outs, and asking where else we could recommend. When it was busy like this, time was elastic. Sometimes thirty minutes felt like two minutes. Other times that same half hour was an age of questions and tight-fistedness from customers. Lou returned and I joined Charles at the rope.

'Who's playing?' a group asked of Charles.

'Eddie B.'

The customers filed in.

'Will you two be OK on the door for a bit? I need a piss and a bit of a break.' Charles asked me.

'Sure. What's your favourite *Star Wars* moment?' I replied.

'OK. I'll give you my number two. *Empire*. Yoda. "Do or do not. There is no try."'

'You gonna send Phil down?'

'Not unless you want me to.'

'Nah, leave him up there. How many have we got?'

'Two-twenty, plus this lot it'll be two-forty. Easy, see ya.' Charles skipped up the stairs leaving me holding the clickers.

I had not done the rope all night. They stood in front of me like hungry cattle.

'Evening folks,' my voice cracked a little.

A chorus of hellos rose.

'We have a pretty full house.'

'Comeonawcomeonpleasepleasewewontbelongpleasecomeon.'

'Ho, ho. Quiet. You—' I pointed at a man in the front of the group. 'What's your number one *Star Wars* moment?' I heard Lou giggle.

'You're joking,' he said.

'Not even a little bit.'

'The battle at the end of *Return of the Jedi* with the ewoks and the rebels against the Empire.'

'The ewoks? Folks you need to find a new venue.'

'Nowayyourjokingthatssounfairican'tbelievethatareyouforrealthatsucks.'

'Sorry guys, we don't have room for you. Try us again another night.'

Grumbling, the group left. All but one. A small man in a red leather jacket and black cargo pants. He stood solitary, staring at the ground in front of my feet. The group paused to my left, audible but out of sight.

'You right mate?'

He looked at me evenly, raised his palm and in a gentle tone said, 'You will let me and my party pass.'

'What?'

'You will let me and my party pass.'

'Whatever, mate.'

'Jedi mind powers.' A smile broke across his face, and mine.

'I'll pay that. Right, you lot, your Jedi friend has saved you, it's five bucks each.'

'Ohyeahniceonerob.'

'Have a good night, folks.'

Lou disappeared in a tsunami of customers clamouring to pay and get to the dance floor.

People kept coming and going. I made some wait, just to practise making them wait. I'd let them in when others left. Other people I let in immediately. Mostly I said no because we were close to our legal capacity. I didn't think about being one of two people and the only man in a dark laneway dealing with hundreds of people who were drunk and on drugs. I didn't think about how isolated we were. I didn't think about not being able to communicate with the main bar upstairs.

At four am, with an hour left till closing, a man wearing a black sleeveless singlet and black silk pants embroidered with small red dragons, came down the stairs. He was muscular and tall. He carried a handbag that didn't match his clothes – it was white leather with thin, expensive-looking handles.

'Excuse me, guys.'

'See you later.'

'See ya.'

Without warning he kissed me on the cheek.

'I'll be back in a minute, just putting this in the car for my girlfriend.'

'Righto. Easy on the kisses.'

'Sure.'

And he was gone.

'Didn't really look gay,' Lou said.

'What about those pants and the hairless arms?'

'Yeah, but he didn't look gay, and he said he had a girlfriend.'

'Mmm. Do you know Charles's number one?'

'Jesus.'

'Do you?'

'Yeah, of course. But I can't tell you. He'd kill me. This is his favourite conversation. I can't ruin his punchline.'

Three minutes later the man in the silk pants was back, without the handbag.

'Hi, guys. OK, if I come back in?'

'Long as you don't kiss me.'

'Sure. Thanks.'

Lou watched him go upstairs.

'Not gay. Definitely. Where the fuck is Charles? He's been gone a half hour.'

'Aren't I doing a good job?'

'You're doing a great job, but we're all alone down here. It's stupid.'

Charles came down the stairs three at a time. He was excited and panting. He ran past Lou and straight to me.

'There's a guy upstairs, taller than you, in a black singlet, and he's wearing tight silk pants.'

'Yeah. He just left, and came back.'

'What? So he left, but he's upstairs again?' Charles looked ready to burst.

'Yeah.'

'If he tries to leave again. Don't let him. He's stolen a purse.'

'He left with a purse, or a handbag.'

'Really? That's it. I'll call you up if I need you.' And he bolted back upstairs. Lou came down to the rope looking confused. 'What's going on?'

'That guy who kissed me, the silk pants man, looks like he stole someone's handbag.'

'The one he was carrying when he left?'

'No. The other one …'

'At least he was stupid enough to come back in.'

'Mmm. And we're stupid enough to accuse him.'

'What do you mean?'

'We're not cops …'

'And he didn't come back with it.' Lou finished my sentence and looked less confused.

'What'll we do?'

'Don't know. Maybe it was a joke. Maybe the customers here are completely different to the people that go to pubs.'

Lou said, 'Maybe we haven't got a leg to stand on and it's a waste of time.'

'Mmm.'

'But, we have to try, don't we?'

'The guys I've worked with would never do anything unless they actually saw the crime.'

Raffie, one of the owners, came down the stairs panting. Forty cigarettes a day and the running of a nightclub were taking their toll. He wheezed, 'Heath, we need you upstairs, in the carpet corridor – now, mate.'

'OK.' I went up the stairs two at a time. Stomach churning. What would be waiting for me? Charles unconscious? Bloody? Dead? The 'Silkpantsman' holding a patron hostage with a broken glass?

I should have asked Raffie. Ten seconds to get from the rope to the double doors. A lot can happen in ten seconds. Luke destroyed the Death Star in less than that. I was scared. This was it. The big moment. The first real bouncer situation at this new job. No Alby. No Anefterios. I was the guy.

Near the double doors Charles was facing the bar, hands up, palms out, talking to Silkpantsman who was taller and had two friends behind him. People were not coming through the doors as they normally did. They knew trouble was brewing.

Over the Navajo chant Charles was saying, 'She said you took it.'

Silkpantsman replied, 'Bullshit, mate. I didn't do anything. Where's your proof?'

'Yeah, mate. You got no fuckin' proof,' chimed one of his friends.

Charles had noticed me and pointing over his shoulder in my direction said, 'This guy saw you leave with the bag.'

They looked past Charles at me and saw my number. There was a pause and Silkpantsman said, 'This is bullshit, I'm leaving.'

He pushed through Charles and into me. Silkpantsman, his friends, Charles and I stumbled together into the lounge. The doors shut behind us and the sound of the dance floor disappeared. The prominent noise now was the grunting and swearing of the five of us as three tried to leave and two tried to stop them. I was trying to establish a wristlock but Silkpantsman, laughing, pulled his arm away each time I tried. Charles was clinging to his other arm and the friends were just walking in time with our rolling wrestle.

Through the doors and to my surprise the man stopped. He pushed Charles and me away but made no attempt to keep leaving. My efforts to control him had been useless. It was a strange position. I had failed to restrain him but he had decided not to go.

'You cunts have got nothing. Weak as fuckin' piss mate, weak as fuckin ...'

In the dim light, I could see his eyes. The pupils were angrily dilated. Black pools rolling around the sockets. His tongue lashed at the sides of his mouth and spilt out of his lips. As coked as they come. He knew we had no grounds or rights to detain him. He was going to stay and enjoy it.

'Call the cops, mate. Go on. What ya got to lose? I'm waitin' for 'em, mate. You pissweak cunts don't even have to try and make me stay. You're so fuckin' sure I done something, call the cops. Show 'em your evidence and they'll take me away. Ring 'em, mate. Go on.'

Everyone in the toilets and chill-out area had escaped into the bar without prompting. Raffie walked in from the bar and I stood at the opening of the corridor that led to the stairs. If I was going to stop him leaving I wanted the least space on either side of me as possible. On my right were the white cane chairs and a glass-topped table. To my left the toilets. Behind me empty space and then four flights of stairs.

Raffie whispered in my ear, 'We're getting everybody out through the fire escape in the bar. Lou is on the door with Philip and I've called the cops. OK?'

I wanted us to tell Silkpantsman that we had no evidence and he was free to go, but I took my lead from Charles. The bar lights were up, people were leaving and the cops were on their way. They wouldn't be long and if the guy was still here, they would deal with it.

'OK,' I muttered.

Charles approached Silkpantsman, who was pacing back and forth across us. His friends were sitting to our left, next to the toilet entrance.

'Mate, we've called the cops. The best thing you can do now is sit down and take it easy. If you didn't pinch the bag, there's nothing for you to worry about and it'll all be sorted in no time.'

'Call the fuckin' cops. Bring 'em on. I got nothing to hide, mate. Nothin'. Bring 'em on. Fuckin' bring 'em on!'

'They're on their way, mate. Don't worry. Why don't you tell us where the bag is and you can go and not have to deal with the police at all?'

'I haven't got the bag, mate. Don't know what you're talking about. You haven't called the cops. You pissweak cunts haven't got the balls to call the cops. They aren't coming. You can't keep us here.'

His eyes fixed on me. He'd lost interest in Charles. In the light, away from the dark of the front door he looked completely different. Not the same guy who bounced out the door and kissed the cheek of a bouncer. He was now more a caged panther than a party boy. I wasn't shaking and my hands weren't sweating but I was terrified. I was also strangely calm. It was an endgame. We had nothing. He had everything. I was going to try and stop him if he tried to leave because that was where I found myself. That was my role in this drama. I had no idea how I'd do it, but I knew it was my task.

'You, ya weak cunt. You reckon you can stop me, do ya? I got two mates with me. What've you got? This other weak as piss dick with a number?'

I said, 'So you keep saying, big fella. You're right. We've got nothing. No evidence and we're weak as piss. We're just hopin' the cops come before you try anything. Otherwise, like you say, we're fucked.'

I'd been knocked out at training, choked into unconsciousness, winded, had kidney punches, a couple of broken ribs and bloody noses. I wasn't afraid of pain. And what was the worst thing that could happen? Another dose of unconsciousness and the guys beating the shit out of every staff member they could find, ransacking the till and burning the place to the ground for a start.

His friends stood up and said, 'We're not stickin' around for any cops, mate. We're outta here. You're on your own with this.'

Then to me and Charles, 'We can leave, yeah? We ain't done nothing. Alright if we go?'

I was about to say, 'Yes, piss off. Two of us on your mate are better odds …'

'Nah. You're all stayin' till the cops get here,' Charles said forcefully.

Thanks Chuck. Keep the odds out of our favour. Nice one.

The two looked at each other. Silkpantsman stared at me. The friends moved away from him to my left. Charles followed them. Silkpantsman and I were face to face. Silkpantsman was big. From nine feet away, I felt like he breathed into my eyes as he said, 'Fuck it. I'm bigger than you.'

He ran at me and to my right. I moved with him, tracking him, leaving a gap between myself and the wall, big enough for him to fit through. I had to be behind him. He charged through the gap on my right. I dove sideways, at full extension, and threw my arm across his throat. His momentum whipped my elbow close around his throat and lurched me forward into the corridor. As my body caught up with his, I wrapped my legs around his waist. He looked over his shoulder and snarled, 'Get off me, cunt.'

'Too late for that, mate.'

My right arm was bent round his throat. I held my left shoulder and crossed my left arm behind his neck. I tightened both left and right arms and cut off the blood to his brain. He carried me down the corridor. One step. Two steps. Three steps. Four – a gurgling noise from his chest. Five steps and he collapsed.

As we fell I pushed off the floor with my feet so the two of us, my arms still tight around his throat, rolled to our right side against the wall. I looked over my left shoulder. One of his mates had knocked Charles over and was running at me. As I hit the floor and the man loomed over me, I kicked up hard with my left leg into his scrotum. He froze. His eyes held on me a moment and then he folded backwards. Charles and Raffie grabbed him and I stopped watching.

Silkpantsman was unconscious in my arms. I relaxed my grip but did not release the hold. Seconds later he sucked in a desperate gasping breath. He thrashed wildly and grabbed at my right arm. I tightened my grip. He couldn't breathe. His brain was starved again of blood and oxygen and he went limp. I relaxed my grip. He breathed. He fought against me and I tightened.

'You will be still, or unconscious. Your choice big guy.'

I was dizzy with adrenalin. He stopped fighting my grip and started talking.

'I'm goin' to kill you. I'm going to fuckin' kill you, mate. When you let me up, I'm gonna kill you. I'll come back here with a knife and I'll cut your eyeballs out. I'll cut your bloody eyeballs out. How's that make you feel, huh? How's it make you feel to know you just killed yourself? You're goin' to die …'

'That's enough.'

I tightened my grip around his throat and a rattle started in his throat. I released the pressure. He whispered, 'Let me go, mate. Come on. Let me go. I don't want to deal with the cops. I just want to go home. I didn't mean to cause trouble. It was all just a joke. Did it for a laugh. Please mate let me go. I'm sorry, alright?'

'Too late.'

'Come on, mate, let me go. Let me go and I'll break you in fuckin' half. I will break you in half and feed your guts to my dog, mate, let me go and I swear to God I'll end it for you.'

'Shut up.'

'Make me, cunt.'

I tightened my arms.

'OK, OK. Let go. Ease up, ease up, fuck. Can you let me go? I swear I'll sit here safe and sound.'

In the space of fifteen seconds I had restrained him and now had his body resting against mine, his back in my lap. We were looking at the space at the top of the stairs, the door to the owners' office and the cigarette machine glowing forever in the corner. He was huge. His weight against my thighs was solid, sweaty and hot.

'Look at ya, what do you weigh?' I asked him.

'What?'

'What do you weigh?'

'Hundred kilos. Hundred and five kilos.'

'See, that's twenty-five, nearly thirty kilos more than me. I'm not going to take you by surprise again, so if I let you up, well, that would just be stupid. The cops will be here any minute. Why don't you just sit back and relax.'

Silkpantsman threw his hips forward and up into the air. The momentum pulled me forward and down over him. His arms raked over the back of my head and grabbed the collar of my T-shirt. He would have been pulling my hair if I had any. I nearly lost my grip on his neck. I tightened hard. I could feel my arms cut in against the edge of his throat. His big body went limp again. I relaxed and waited. Again he revived.

I felt good sitting in the corridor with a one-hundred-kilo disco bunny in a guillotine choke. I was untouchable, unbreakable, golden. A Luke Skywalker moment. Whether the owners were upset about the course of events or not wouldn't matter. I hadn't created the situation, but I had cleaned it up. I had finished what should not have been started. Fuck Luke, I felt like Obi Wan.

The police eventually came. They walked in the door followed by Lou and Philip and walked straight past me. They went down the corridor and talked with the owners. They took statements from the two friends and eventually relieved me. I had been sitting there for forty minutes. Silkpantsman didn't turn to look at me.

Silkpantsman's friends gave him up without prompting. The policeman in charge explained that Silkpantsman admitted stealing the bag and was going to lead them to it. He would be charged. The woman whose bag it was came to the club regularly for the next two years but never thanked Charles or me.

When the police left with the three men, I walked back through the club. Busboys were cleaning up, rolling tall green bins full of beer stubbies and used-up citrus sections into the lift. I moved through the chill-out zone, empty and quiet. Just the faint chant of the Indian playing through the speakers.

'Heath.'

Charles and Lou were behind the bar. Behind them, glistening in the full force of the house lights bottles of spirits were the only things in the place that looked shiny and new. The floor was marked with cigarette burns, the fur surfaces of the couches were worn bare and everyone looked exhausted, but the light kept bouncing through those bottles.

'Yeah?' I moved over to the bar. They had been cuddling, consoling each other.

'How are you?' Charles asked.

'Fine, shoulder hurts, but not too bad.'

Charles went on, 'I probably owe you an apology.'

'Why?'

'That wasn't the most well-handled situation.'

'No, you don't. I reckon it's good we took a stand. Had a happy ending. None of us are injured, no patrons are injured, no ambulances. Has to be a good thing.'

'You will be still or you will be unconscious.' Lou smiled as she repeated my line and asked, 'Did you rehearse that?'

'Pretty cheesy, huh? I don't know where that came from.'

'Or the kick to the nuts as you choked out the first guy. That was pretty inspired,' Charles added.

'I'm going home, guys. Say goodbye to Philip and Raffie for me.'

'Sure,' they chimed.

As I walked away Charles called, 'Hey, second half of *Empire*. Darth knocks Luke into the freeze tank, but Luke leaps out as the carbon gas churns out and turns on his lightsaber. Darth says, "Impressive … most impressive."'

Chapter 23

IMPRESSIVE ... MOST IMPRESSIVE

IT HAD BEEN A VIOLENT SITUATION, ONE THAT A YEAR OR TWO EARLIER WOULD have frozen me with terror. Now, through experience and training, I had controlled chaos and bent it to my will. Bouncing calls for decisiveness and clear parameters. In the rest of my life there were no clear delineations between right and wrong. Everything was in degrees. Now, what I had sensed existed in the life of a bouncer that first night in the Royal I had found.

While I was working I knew what was right and what was not and I had the mandate to enforce that code of behaviour. I didn't need to negotiate or validate myself with words. I could state the parameters and enforce them if necessary but I'd seen how Alby and Anefterios were oblivious to talking. It's not the words we are listening to. We're waiting for a subliminal sign that the person we're dealing with understands and respects our position and power. Once that's observed they can talk for hours but the words are only noise. I don't have to hear or remember their name or what they do for a living. I only need to know that they know who I am and what I do. That's what matters.

At work later that week, cold in the laneway, I got a call. I could hear the familiar sounds of the Royal down the line.

'Hey, grasshopper.'

'Terry?'

'Yeah, mate. Hear you're the new kid on the block.'

'What do you mean?'

'Shut up, dickhead. Stepped up, mate. Good on ya. Wasn't sure you had it in ya, mate, but sounds like ya did real good.'

'Thanks, Terry. Did Alby tell you?'

'Whaddaya reckon? You have a good night, mate, gotta go to work.'

A few weeks later I was training with Alby in the church hall. Pigeon shit on the floor and used furniture lining the walls. A couple of other zealots were there for the morning session and Alby worked us into the ground. By eleven o'clock we stood repeating a series of arm and hand drills, each dripping sweat that spread out in stains on the floorboards. When we finished and were standing about exhausted but high with endorphins, Alby announced, 'We gotta leave the hall. They're gonna renovate so we gotta go.'

'Where to?' asked Lee.

'I found a warehouse round the corner. It's pretty big. Have to get some people living in there, maybe some of you guys, but the hall upstairs is perfect. What about going on the lease with me, and you can manage the place, keep guys in there in line and have a studio and start teaching a few classes every week?'

'Seriously?'

'Yeah.'

Could it get any better? I felt like I had graduated as a bouncer and now I was going to live and teach in our new kung fu school. I floated through the day and in the evening prepared myself for work.

A long, hot shower, finished with a freezing blast for as long as I could bear. A close shave. Black jeans and a black T-shirt, long-sleeved black top and a denim jacket. Warm socks. Grey trainers. I packed my backpack: muesli bars, nuts, a book, a martial arts magazine and an energy drink. Beanie, always a beanie. Say goodbye to the dog. She wonders again why I'm going out at night. Bike. Shut the door. I love this drill.

Wheeling down the lane to the club I could hear Charles's voice and Raffie's laughter. A couple, beautiful and young, walked towards me.

'Don't bother, mate, they're fuckin' arseholes. Have to be a bloody prince or movie star to get in. Wankers.'

I grunted and smiled to myself. I would never get in if I wasn't working there. I'd never cared for nightclubs before, but now I felt that I belonged, not because I was beautiful or cool, but, because I was the perfect bouncer for the club.

I rounded the corner. Charles and Raffie stood on the inside of the rope. Hugh stood outside it, pretending to be a rejected customer.

'Aw come on, guys, let me in. I just have to get in. It's really important. Really important. Like my girlfriend is up there and if I don't get up there she's gonna fuck my best friend. Guys, come on.'

I smelt the joint Hugh was smoking. I stood behind him and said to Charles, 'He's alright. He's with me.'

Hugh turned and with red eyes said, 'Thank you, sweetheart.'

'Pleasure.'

'Thanks heaps for the other night,' Hugh said.

I took a moment and said, 'Just doin' my job, eh.'

'Listen to this guy. Where did you find him, Charles! Just doin' my job. You practise that line or what? Anyway, look we want to offer you a permanent job and a pay rise. Twenty-five an hour, how's it sound?'

'Well, great. Sounds great. Thanks.'

'No problem,' Raffie said as he pulled deeply on the joint.

'I'm ah, goin' upstairs to sign on. Thanks again.'

The bar staff met me with adulation. The patrons slapped my back and told those who had not been there what I'd done. I was un-comfortably aware that I was the sole topic of conversation. I hurried to sign on, get a lemonade and go downstairs. In other people's retelling, the event sounded dramatic. Hearing my actions in other people's mouths, I understood that aggression was now the basis for my identity. I was the tough-guy bouncer.

On Monday Alby and I went to a nice big office in the middle of the city and signed a three-year lease on our warehouse.

The warehouse was immense. Two floors of over six hundred square feet. Two-thirds of the ground floor was taken up by large offices that we were going to use as bedrooms, a living room and a small kitchen. The rest of the floor was less civilised and would be roughly partitioned and used as artists' studios. This area had a roller door onto the street and double metal doors onto a blue stone laneway at the back. There was a staircase on one wall that led upstairs. The ground floor was very dark, with a low ceiling. Natural light was scarce and all but two of the five bedrooms were windowless.

Upstairs was completely different. In place of a cold cement floor it had squeaky polished boards and a huge vaulted ceiling. At each end of the floor was a bank of three windows. Each window was made up of nine sixty-centimetre square panes in steel frames. They faced roughly north–south so the training area was always bathed in sunlight but never glary. On the west side of the upper floor a door led to a balcony that was at the top of a staircase leading down to street level. The balcony had a beautiful view up the hill to the Victorian building that was a supermarket.

The building was in a sad state. The brick walls sagged and swayed. The concrete sheet ceiling showered us with dust. We moved some of Alby's bigger sculptures into the hall to give it character. Two huge wooden hands holding carved landscapes and ocean scenes. Each stood twelve feet tall. The cane staffs we used for weapons practice were held in place by two carved grizzly bears each one eight-feet high. The floor groaned under the weight of these monsters but we trusted. It took days to make them presentable. My bedroom was the only room on this upper floor besides the training hall and the toilets. I had windows that looked out onto the street. The street was depressing when seen from above. The only people that passed our building were inhabitants of the high-rises and during the day it was only the drug-dependent ones that walked by, screaming at each other about which prick owed what in fags or stereos until a half hour later they sauntered by pinned to the eyeballs and in love with one another again.

Our warehouse was dwarfed by the building directly across the road from it – the Wellington Street housing commission high-rise, and three-hundred metres down the road its sibling on Hoddle Street. Our building was fifty metres from a small intersection with a milk bar and a Vietnamese greasy spoon. The shops had steel bars on all windows and doors and closed at four o'clock. When night fell it was dangerous to venture any further into the housing complex than these shops.

Both Lee and I loved the warehouse and everything about it. It made us feel alive to be near danger. Lee and the guys read true crime stories about Chopper Read and other local goons while they waited for a turn on the PlayStation. Someone was always just coming home from work or just about to leave and if you were home for a while, you'd always stop in the living area downstairs. The PlayStation was always on. The first effort of the warehouse kitty was to pool together and buy a PlayStation 2.

When we weren't working, eating or sleeping, we were training. Lee and I had a weekly rendezvous outside class time with friends from other clubs, where we would train in pairs, hitting bags or each other. Alby constructed a frame of oregon beams and hung twelve punching bags from them. They groaned like the hull of some great ship as we pounded them. My collection of skipping ropes were slung up in a corner and the whipping sound of a rope was almost always heard. Eventually Alby bought some interlocking foam mats and covered half of the floor with them so we could fight and wrestle.

Some of us had girlfriends, but the warehouse had a way of making women who weren't there to train feel a little uncomfortable. Of four or five guys who lived there, only Lee's relationship survived and that was because early on his girlfriend saw that this was something she was just going to have to wait out.

Somehow we managed to keep three dogs in the warehouse. The dogs soon learned to piss and shit on the downhill slope of the car park just inside the roller door. We were careful to clean the area at least once a week, but it was something we became a little desensitised to – the looks of alarm on the faces of visitors somehow became a surprise to us. The place was a temple to testosterone. There was no room for anything feminine. And if there had been it would have been killed off by the fortnightly sluicing with hospital bleach we gave the place.

Our favourite neighbour was Toothy. He lived in one of the two-storey housing commission terraces that huddled in the shadow of the high-rise. A salivating malamute patrolled Toothy's porch. It was the biggest and most tormented dog I had ever seen. It was never walked, and never off the chain. Toothy himself was a short and portly figure. He always wore stubby shorts and a ragged blue singlet. His hair was curly and lank, his arms were a smudge of bad tattoos and he had no front teeth.

Cars would arrive at Toothy's place of an evening. After midnight, without lights, Toothy and one or two others would descend on the cars like locusts and by morning, all that would be left were steel frames and a couple of hub caps.

The RSPCA came a few times to try and rescue the dog. Toothy would simply stand at the door and yell in his toothy way, 'Fug uth ya thunts. Va fuggin dug fuggin nuvs id. Oo come an ake im avay. Iv ee goes wiv youse, youse can vuggi ave im, now fug uth ya thunts!'

One Sunday morning Lee and I watched as fifteen armed policeman surrounded the house, sedated the dog and entered the building. They came out a short time later with Toothy in handcuffs, carried by six coppers as he screamed, 'VER AL MA FUGGIN HARS YA FUGGIN THUNTS. I GO VA THUGGIN PAPERTH FOR THUGGIN ALL O VEM YOU FIFTY THNEAKY THTINKIN THUNTS.'

Toothy was replaced by a Vietnamese family who ran a hairdressing service. Where Toothy had kept a malamute they kept succulents in heavy cement containers.

Chapter 24
CHARLES LEAVES

CHARLES LANDED A JOB DESIGNING INTERIORS FOR AN ARTS FESTIVAL somewhere in Queensland. He talked about coming back to the club but he hadn't been himself in the weeks since the silkpantsman. We wouldn't see him again, as an employee.

His departure left a security staff of only Philip and me. Philip would only work upstairs. This meant that I was the door bitch and enforcer all rolled into one, backed up by Lou, the money girl, Raffie on Friday when he was sober, and Johnny on Saturday when he actually showed up at the door. Most Saturday nights he came in the front of the building through a small door near the bar and we barely saw him.

I could manage the door. But it was not unusual to have a hundred people waiting to get in, while nearly three hundred fought for air and drinks upstairs. Having only one person on security who could be relied on to remain sober as well as intervene in a violent situation was unsustainable. The solution the owners came up with was Floyd. He looked as Greek as a steaming, oven-baked slab of haloumi with olive oil and rosemary but maintained he was of Liverpuddlian heritage. A lovely guy, he was my size and enigmatic in a kind, monosyllabic way. He did karate, smoked and drank.

We got together after our first night on duty to spar. He brought a full kit of pads: shin, foot, head, chest and big gloves. I came with a skipping rope and a pair of padded fingerless bag mitts. He saw my lack of accessories and matched me with only gloves. We warmed up separately. I skipped; he did some kata. Then we faced up. The first thing I did was kick his leading thigh because it was so heavily planted it was going to take him a week to get it out of the way.

'Fuck!'

'Shit, sorry, what?' I asked

'Didn't know you were going to kick legs.'

'I just thought … from the karate I've seen. Sorry.'

'We only kick above the waist.'

'Lotta good that's gonna do in your line of work.'

He just looked at me. I felt rude. We agreed on some ground rules – no kicking below the waist – and faced up again. He feigned a jab with his left hand. Once, twice and a third time. The third time I swatted it to my left with my right hand. Away from him. His left hand was down. I stepped in slightly with my right foot and hit him with a back fist. He had a brown belt in karate. That's pretty high. I expected him to block my punch and hadn't thought much past that but he didn't.

'Fuck!'

He clasped his face.

'Shit, sorry.'

He recovered but we didn't spar any more. He was good-natured about it, and didn't mind when I nicknamed him Lightning. It was good to have another body around but he was always grumpy or tucked away inside the big door chatting to Lou so my anxiety about the door was not allayed.

The paradox of our door policy was that people's subjective judgements were so often right. Nerdy groups of men with pocket protectors and satchel bags did tend to occupy large seating areas, drinking one beer every two hours. Men in denim shirts, chinos and boating loafers did drink a lot of beer, become rowdy and breathily ask darling what her name was, what's with the funny outfit and did she wanna go suck cock. Giggling groups of eighteen-year-olds went upstairs, dropped ecstasy and danced all night, refilling their water bottles in the toilets. And muscular, tanned and hairless Mediterranean men would remove their shirts on the dance floor, drink a lot and eventually lean over the bar and shirtcollar the barman. Hens' and bucks' nights would end the evening covering walls, floors and themselves in bilious sprays of vomit.

What people wore and how they looked were the criteria we used for selection, but it worked. The problem was that making the selection criteria acceptable to these people called for diplomatic skills I could muster only in short bursts.

'I could do it,' Lou said defiantly, halfway through another night collecting money. 'And get paid a damn sight more than I do now!'

She was right and we resolved to talk about with an owner as soon as we found one.

Chapter 25
THE GUN

Officially, Johnny was on the door with me on Saturdays. He would generally excuse himself to go upstairs after half an hour and that would be the last I saw of him. That was fine with me. Johnny had a habit of interrupting me as I was getting rid of a group, and overruling my decision. This most often happened when a member of the party possessed large and visible breasts. As an owner he could do as he bloody well pleased.

I had surrendered the door to his control and Lou was eying me to raise the idea of her as door bitch. A group of three came to the fence, two men and one woman. They looked wrong. Shifty eyes, long sleeves on a hot night, challenge in their posture. Johnny stood close to the fence. I hated that he did this. It meant there was no distance for an attacker to cover, and he pissed off so many potential customers by being so obviously biased towards breasts I was amazed he hadn't been slugged yet. He whispered in his tiny tones at the three that it was a full house and they would need to be members. They asked for clarification.

He replied, 'Look, guys, as I said, it's a full house so we aren't letting anyone in without members' passes. I won't be able to help you tonight.'

'You sure, mate? I've been really wanting to check this place out. Sure you can't help us?'

There was threat in his voice but Johnny didn't hear it.

'No, mate. Sorry, can't do it.'

Two women, in singlet tops, breasts brimming, approached.

'Evening ladies.'

He opened the rope and let them through.

'Where's their members' pass, mate. Didn't see them flashing anything 'cept their tits.'

'They're friends of mine.'

'Bullshit.'

I tugged the back of Johnny's shirt to get him away from the fence. He ignored me. He didn't see the anger building in the dark-haired man. The guy stood close to Johnny and I stayed as near as I could. I wanted to clip Johnny across the back of the head.

Johnny tried to explain, 'Look, buddy, what can I say …'

The guy spat in Johnny's face. I punched the guy in the nose. Johnny reeled away to my left, and as he was jolted backwards by my fist the man pulled his right hand out of his jacket pocket, pointing a small, silver gun at me. I turned to my right and as I ran in under the doorframe I scooped Louise up. I threw her down the fire escape and in two steps had gone up a flight and a half of stairs. I turned and looked through the corner of the stairs, my body hidden by the next flight. Lou was squatting in the fire escape ashen and hyperventilating. The man was at the door, still on the far side of the fence. He was pointing the gun in my direction.

'Come on, ya fuckin' coward cunt. Come and hit me, now, ya fuckin' coward. Ya cunt. I'll put fuckin holes in you, mate. Come on. Yeah, ya fuckin' yellow.'

His voice was nasal, whining. He waved the gun at me a little longer and walked up the laneway. I ran around the fence and yelled at him as he walked away that if he would like to put the gun away I would quite happily kill him. I repeated this a couple of times for effect and returned to my side of the swaying picket fence.

Johnny had been sheltering behind the wall that was a doorway to the elevator. Lou came out of the fire escape.

'Everyone alright?'

'Yep.'

It had taken less than thirty seconds from the spitting to the leaving. It was over. I couldn't remember the guy's face. All I could remember was that he was wearing a blue slicker and had greasy black hair. I wouldn't know him if he came back. Suddenly, there were people at the rope who had not seen the incident and Johnny had gone upstairs to clean his face. I was back on the job.

'Hi, guys. Come in. Five dollars.'

And so the night continued. I felt like I was dreaming. Everywhere I looked I saw the little, black, plughole pupil of the weapon pointed at me. Sometimes big, darkening my field of vision; sometimes tiny, like a sunspot. Louise sensibly suggested that we shut the door and call the police, in case he came back. I said he wouldn't come back. I just didn't want to stop and think. I wanted everything to keep going so I could avoid facing the truth of what had just happened.

Chapter 26
AFTER THE GUN

THE WEEK AFTER THE GUN WAS EUPHORIC. EVERY BREATH I TOOK ELECTRIFIED me, lit me up, sent delicious searing beams of light through my body. At work I was a benevolent god. I could see the bigger picture, we were all a family and we needed to love one another. I was patient with customers and healed lepers on my break. For a sweet week my mortality was a natural high.

After closing the next Saturday night I took home the CCTV recording of the incident. On Tuesday I put it in the machine at home. The grainy, over-exposed view of the club's entrance came up on the screen. I recognised the date. Johnny and I were on the screen. Lou was walking back and forth, in and out of frame in her outrageous miniskirt. Patrons were at the fence that cut the screen in half, top to bottom. After a couple of seconds the view cut to the bar's teeming throng. Cut to the entrance. Three people walked on screen from the laneway at the right of frame. Cut to the bar. I didn't see him immediately, hidden as he was between the girl and the other guy. They approached the fence and began the actions I remembered. It was haunting seeing it in black and white, without sound. It needed a score. Cut to the bar again, on the webcam. Back at the entrance it looked like Johnny was having a conspiratorial word in the guy's ear and then we all moved as friends, calmly, to the fence. Busy bar. I stood back and leaned against the wall. The bar again. The guy's two companions took freeze-frame steps backwards as Johnny leaned a little further over the fence. The bar. I stepped forward, the guy appeared to sneeze; his phlegm invisible in the grainy image. My hand went from my side to his nose. The bar. The gun. The bar. I was shepherding Lou inside out of frame. Other customers on his side of the fence evaporated. Cut to the bar. He stood alone in camera except for Johnny tucked in the top left-hand corner of the screen, half hidden by a brick pillar.

The guy on screen waving the gun in silence. The gun kept disappearing in the poor resolution of the screen. Bar. He was off up the lane, out of shot, and I was in frame. Bar. I was out from behind the rope and in the lane. The bar. No one in frame except for Johnny hiding and wiping spit from his face. No screaming, no shouting, no rushing, no colour. Busy bar. Empty lane. Bar. Empty lane. Bar. Empty lane. Bar. Me walking back into frame, alone. Silent. Pale.

The tape broke away to a snowstorm and I returned to my body, sucked in a breath and shuddered. I watched the twenty-five seconds from just before he spat to when I walked back into frame over and again, perhaps forty or fifty times. The same grainy sequence, over and over. It was all so quick. So much happened between frames. So many things we should or should not have done. I watched the video all week. I showed it to Alby and he told me I had done the right thing, that anyone would run from a gun and so they should, and that I was right to whack a guy for spitting in my employer's face.

I showed my dad, and he didn't say anything. I showed friends and they asked if I had quit yet. I didn't show my mum.

I was looking for a response from someone that would calm the tempest inside me. I could hear people telling me I had done the right thing but could not accept it. I knew it was madness to stay in such a situation but I had felt so good recently.

On Friday night Philip came in. He hadn't been there when it happened. He hadn't seen the video. He'd heard about the incident, though, and told me I'd done the wrong thing. I should never have touched the guy and by doing so, I should assume responsibility for all the consequences.

That was what I was looking for – the green light to blame myself. After Silkpantsman it had all been so smooth. I had been untouchable. But after the gun incident, something that should have shattered my delusions of omnipotence, I had felt even better. I stood at the door all that night asking myself the questions my mum might have asked.

'What if you had been shot?'

'Why did you chase the guy up the lane?'

'What if the guy had come around the fence and found everyone?'

'What if the guy had come back?'

'What if someone had died?'

'What if you had died?'

Eight hours later I went home and didn't sleep a wink. I drifted through Saturday without eating and went to work again at ten o'clock. Haunted.

I got home at five-thirty. I climbed into bed. Catherine, a young woman whom I had been seeing over the last few weeks, was there asleep and I watched the rise and fall of her ribs. Fragments of a dawn still an hour away were creeping in between the window and curtain and falling on her skin. I followed the line of her spine with my hand from the top of her neck down to her lower back and rested on the flat bit of body that was the plain before the hills of her buttocks. Sleep was further away now and I turned my hand down, pressing my palm in between her cheeks. I started to play with her and before long I could see her breathing shift and knew she was awake. Quivers moved over her skin like a squall. Minutes later, without a word spoken, I was kneeling behind her grunting and sweaty.

In these pre-dawn mismatched matings she was quiet and disoriented as I let go of the night's playreel of sexy snapshots – snatched visions of sweaty cleavage, toilet cubicle fellatio, tonguey slurping kisses, the eyes of a young woman rolled back in blind ecstasy as a nameless, faceless man gulped at her throat, arses grinding against each other on the dance floor, women snaking up and down men in dark corners, the inside of a woman's thigh, too high, seen as she turned on a bar stool, breasts pressed together swaying over the rope, orgasms repeated all night to house music.

As I approached my climax, I became aware of the woman I was actually with. I looked down at her arse, to the point where we met, the wet interface of two bodies, closed my eyes again, and saw myself on the bed cut open and bloody, crying to her for help as I was dying. Breath bubbling in a wide-open wound of curdled blood and skinless ribcage.

I shook myself free of the vision, squeezed her and heard her groan gently. I came back to my body. I felt sweat running down my back and over my tailbone. I looked down. My chest was whole and sealed.

I was lying on a road watching as a bus drove over me. All six or eight wheels went over my head and my skull popped like a melon. Blood and brain porridge ran from my shaking body into the gutter and passengers peered back at my headless shuddering figure. I watched the sun dry the blood and the arrival of flies. Bits of brain cooked on the hot bitumen.

Again I shook myself. Opened my eyes. Catherine was lying on the bed on her back. A line of light fell across her breasts and I was grateful for her beauty and for sunlight. She was staring at me quizzically. I had no idea how long we had been separated from each other. I was still kneeling, but now without her, and sweat was cooling on my back.

'What happened?' she asked.

'I died.'

'Apparently.' She giggled.

'No, I mean in my head. I thought it was summer and I was on the road and a bus … I thought I died.'

'Are you OK, sweetheart?'

'I guess so. I'm still here … I suppose.'

The radiance and ecstasy of the first days after the gun were gone.

Now I was waking in fright, never sure if I had dreamt a death or lived one. It was harrowing and always a shock, leaving me sweating and adrenalised. There was no going back to sleep once the dreams began. It would only mean a return to a more violent, more graphic reliving of the same death or a new and more terrible one. As my sleep diminished, the visions began to creep into my waking hours.

There came a point where the visions began, but I failed to recognise it until something jolted me from its grip. I would find myself returned to a complete and working body, disoriented and afraid. I stopped at a red light, but the car rolled into the junction, into the path of oncoming traffic. My tiny Honda ricocheted from car to car, into poles, into buildings. My head and body were thrown around the car, pinned by the seatbelt.

My collarbones shattered and the ligaments tore, my femurs and fibulas cracked and compressed into one another and erupted through my flesh like arrows. The car I hit continued like the bow of a great icebreaker, driving through the dashboard, smashing my legs into my lap, up through my chest and carrying my head and neck with it into the back seat. It pounded my little car from one collision to the next like a kid's ball, spinning and wildly gaining momentum with each new impact. My body lay in pieces amid the wreckage and my mind climbed like a raven picking up pieces of detail: bone, tissue, smells and the reactions of onlookers.

The traffic lights changed to green and the driver behind tooted, stirring me. Off I drove, safely, through the intersection and on to some new nightmare.

No routine was safe from these visions. There was no respite. My raging mind found me dead, bloody, broken but lucid in hundreds of settings. It was never painless. If it came from behind I always got to see it coming at the last moment and witness its full terror. Strangely, I was never shot. My deaths always involved the breaking of my body, the crushing or smashing of my trunk, decapitation, being knee-capped by the bonnet of a car, watching as a motorbike drove into my side at full speed, ceilings collapsing on top of me or, trains derailing and crushing me. And it never happened quickly. I got to see it all, from every angle.

I watched as each detail of my destruction played out, viscerally, over and over and over again.

It started to happen at work. Driving, shopping, walking the dog were settings I could cope with. But at work there was no retreat. Unless I locked myself in a toilet cubicle, there was nowhere I could hide the rivers of sweat or the terror in my eyes.

The visions were more sinister at work too. People were more dangerous, not just observers of my plight but malevolent participants. I would go for a piss and it would happen. I would be lying on the floor of the toilet on my back, spraying piss everywhere and at the same time trying to shield myself from the shoes raining down on me, splintering my ribs and crushing my organs, and as I gasped for air and grasped for a urinal to haul myself up on, the crowd would take out their cocks and hose my wounds with urine. Then someone would say something that roused me. I would turn quickly to the sink and wash my hands, rinse my face and walk out of the room.

After telling a patron they couldn't take the beer glass with them, they threw the drink in my face and as the brew filled my nose and eyes I felt the glass rim hit the bridge of my nose, shatter and cut through the flesh of my face. Glass slivers sliced my eyes and the gristle of my nose. I would taste beer and blood, cocktailed with glass shards running briney down my throat.

'Sorry mate, can I finish it here and leave the glass?'

'Sure.'

When I refused entry, I would feel the impact of the patron's punch and the bouncing of my brain in its delicate puddle, the second punch driving me back and off-balance. As I fell to the ground the man would mount me, straddling my chest and, like a schoolyard pageant, the crowd would watch as he punched every detail out of my face. Then I would find myself talking to the next customer as my imagined assailant walked rejected around the corner.

I couldn't tell anyone. I tried a few times, but choked on the confession. My fear was that if I revealed what was happening to me, I would lose any control I had over it. That other people would think me silly was my greatest comfort, it kept me attached to the truth that my visions were loathsome fantasies. As long as I felt embarrassed by my multiple deaths, then they remained a survivable torture. If someone had told me that they were valid and that I should honour them in any way, I think I would have disintegrated under the weight of them.

One Sunday afternoon when the sun was shining, I was walking by the river after three weeks of falling off cliffs and being hit by cars. I saw some sense and took a fortnight off work.

I slept. I ignored the dog. Eventually she stopped nuzzling me for food or attention and settled for joining me on the bed. I ignored my friends. I turned my mobile off, and didn't return any of the post-it messages my housemates stuck in layers on my door.

Housemates made daring morning sorties into my room to rescue glasses. Visitors came and went, but the guys warned them from entering my room. Catherine visited briefly but soon understood she had no place in that room, at that time. My mother may have dropped by at some stage.

Through it all I slept. I rose only to drink water and to scavenge from the fridge. At first my sleep was tormented, but after two days, broken sleep gave way to real, recuperative slumber. I slept the sleep of the dead. If I dreamt, I had no memory of it. If I woke I only had to listen for the air filling my lungs and leaving again and I was soon away again in peaceful rest. My body and mind had conspired to keep me in bed and now they grasped their opportunity to regroup and recover with great force.

My room began to stink. The curtains were never drawn nor the windows opened. With my breath, the dog's breath, my farts and the dog's farts, the air was foul. The sheets were greasy and when the afternoon sun forced its way in through a crack in the curtains a smelly, sticky steam rose from my futon. Food scraps dried and festered or were licked at noisily by the dog from plates by my bed.

Eat, sleep. Eat, sleep. Eat, sleep went the pistons. My housemates accepted my retreat and began to prepare larger meals. The fridge always held a container of this or that. I would look out the windows at a grey smear of dawn, or a trawling orange dusk, an inky night or an afternoon of terracotta peaks and the soaring monolith of the commission flats while munching on cold rogan josh, or farfalle and pesto. I chewed through ice cream containers full of roast vegetables and couscous with scoops of yogurt or tahini. Cold sausages caked in opaque and salty grease. Hand after hand of bananas and bag upon bag of fleshy, friendly mandarins.

I never heated anything; it was fast, functional eating. Fridge to bowl to mouth to belly to bowel to bowl and back to bed. That my warehouse mates respected my need for food and solitude helped me more than I knew at the time. I was deeply affected by that man pointing a gun at me and calling me a coward. It had made me lonely, cut me off from the world. I needed now only to be alone and cared for quietly.

Chapter 27

NEVILLE

AFTER SLEEPING FOR THE BETTER PART OF TWO WEEKS I WENT INTO WORK FOR a meeting with the owners.

'I want some back-up guys. I want a couple of Samoans the size of cars standing behind me at the door. Otherwise I'll probably be leaving.'

'Oh, hey. Whoa there, mate. Let's not get ahead of ourselves.'

'Yeah, man. Let's talk about this.'

I wanted to scream that I wasn't going to talk about it. I wanted to shout, 'Fuck you for joking.' I wanted to throw furniture and pull guns from my bag and shove them into their mouths and press their heads to the desk and shout, 'What do you think of this, funny men,' so they would piss themselves and apologise and understand and do everything I asked. But that was just the nerves thinking. By the end of the meeting I was reassured. Raffie was going to find out about some agencies and we would meet with their managers during the week. I would help with the decision. They referred to me as their Security Manager.

The first meeting took place the next Tuesday. I came in at midday to meet with AAA security.

Daylight made the club look cheap and ill-considered. The floor was pockmarked with cigarette burns and the carpet was sticky. The couches were tired and seedy. The pony-fur pillows were worn to shiny. At night the mirrors and glass mobiles refracted lights into rainbows, but without coloured light and the veil of night they were the detritus of a high school art room. The Vietnamese plastic foliage on the ceiling didn't look eclectic, postmodern or clever. It looked sad.

The same was true of the owners. Hugh and Raffie were at the club when I arrived.

'Hey, Heathy.'

'Gents.'

Raffie was wearing Birkenstocks and custom-made pants in a modern fabric. His shirt was a black thermal sweater with red details. He had a two-week beard and wore a thin, leather collar necklace. He was drinking a tall glass of juice, smoking and coughing. He looked comfortable when he smoked, but his skin was tired. Hugh was wearing a bright pink tennis visor and sunglasses with aerodynamic, oil slick lenses above his chunky prescription frames. His hair stood out the top of his cap, electric and mad. His pants were slippery and sshhhed together when he moved his legs. They had a sequined butterfly on the left calf. He wore an expensive pair of slip-ons and a baby blue jacket. He looked fantastic. These guys had survived a weekend of hosting and toasting. I had had twenty hours' sleep in the last four nights. My tongue was stuck to my palette and my eyes were sweating. I was wearing pyjamas. A cotton top and zip-up athletic sweater with a pair of martial arts trousers.

Hugh drank half a can of coke in one go, lit a cigarette, popped the top off a can of Japanese iced coffee and said, 'Heathy, we had our usual weekly meeting and we feel we need an increased female presence on the door. We want to get Louise to start doing the selections.

That will mean you can back her up, but you won't have to do all the talking, and then this agency guy will be the back-up for you. Sound alright?'

'Sounds great.'

'Really?'

'Yeah. I'm not door bitch material. I can cover the door, but you need someone with flair and charisma doing that job.'

'Mate, don't be so hard on yourself. You're charismatic.'

'Whatever. Have you floated the idea with Lou?'

'Yeah, she's on board. We also feel we need someone upstairs with Philip.'

'What, you mean someone upstairs who's not off their face?'

'Put bluntly.'

'Great idea.'

'Can you think of anyone, maybe someone from that private army you call your martial arts club?'

'I know just the guy. I'll see if he's up for it.'

They had changed my job without consulting me. It annoyed the shit out of me. But having some help upstairs, especially if it was Lee, would be a relief. Raffie's phone rang.

'No worries. Come up the stairs. I'll open the door for you.'

Raffie returned from the door with Nev. I was introduced as the Security Manager.

Nev was my height but carried more weight. His hair was snow blond and stuck out in little gelled spikes. Eyes ablaze. His face was chubby and his neck a buoyant pillow above his collar. His slacks fitted badly and his shoes had an inch and a half of heel. He wore a black bomber jacket, a dirty white shirt and an ugly tie. His mouth moved constantly.

Nev shook hands firmly with us all and sat himself in the middle of the horseshoe bench. Me on his left, Raffie on his right. Hugh sat apart, straight backed, with his cigarette burning.

Nev began. 'Here's a publicity pack I get the girls to put together for prospective clients. You'll find a description of what we can do, what we've done, how we did it, where it was, what happened to the clientele and the response of the establishment. You'll see we're a firm with twenty-three and a half years' experience in the industry in all aspects of security, bodyguarding, static security, residential, valuables transfer, courts, and of course the hospitality industry, which, let's face it, is the bread and butter for most of us these days. We can provide as many men as you need, all fully qualified and licenced. Any questions?'

'Not yet,' Raffie replied.

'Let you know a little about myself. Started working security when I was seventeen, joined the army, officer's training in ninety-four. Went to the States, did a few years' work and trained as a bodyguard, came back here. Did a year or two in security before starting this business. We provide our own insurance and if there is ever a need for more guys at short notice, we're only a phone call away, fellas, a phone call away. Look at the handouts in your own time, 'cos your time is valuable and so is mine. We can discuss things, cover what you're looking for and then I'll be on my way and you can have a talk and get back to me. I'm a phone call away, always a phone call away. How many floors is the place?'

'One. This is it.' And the front entrance, downstairs in the laneway.

'Shit! Sorry, mate. I thought you were a whole lot bigger. Where do the patrons enter? Is it where I came in?'

'No. The other end of the building,' I said.

Nev was getting sticky spittle spots at the corners of his mouth.

'Righto. What are you looking for? Why did you ring us? What can we do for you?'

'Heathy, do you want to do this?'

Raffie had called me Heathy. My credibility was shot. Nev and I assessed each other. I had him pegged as a psycho. Anti-union and chest deep in the far right. He'd have me as a uni student or dropout, in the industry by accident and not a 'real' bouncer. My comfortable clothes and five-day growth would not harden my image. I was grateful Philip wasn't there.

'Sure. We're getting more popular. Turning away more people and we're getting more trouble.'

'And you need more back-up. No worries, look, that's just the beginning of the service our guys provide. When you hire guys through us, they'll be happy to do the door, back each other up, move around upstairs. The guys we employ are ready to do everything that needs to be done in a bar like this.'

'That's a little more than we would be needing them to do. We have three in-house staff on each night and …'

'How many upstairs? How many on the door?'

'Philip upstairs. Me and one of the owners downstairs.'

'You do the door by yourself, or with one of these guys?'

'Yep.'

Nev reviewed his assessment of me.

I continued, 'We've had a couple of incidents lately … We need a visual presence. A really big guy who can change peoples' minds before they have a go.'

'No worries. Look, we did this down at the Derby, off Mark Street. They had another company there and the guys were letting anyone in. We came and inside a month there was no one there that had been coming when we took over.'

'Were the management happy with that?' Hugh asked.

'We totally cleaned it up. Sent guys in that don't put up with nonsense or silliness, and they got results.'

Raffie and Hugh wanted nonsense and silliness. The sillier a night the more successful. They had bottom-lit surfaces in the women's cubicles for just the sort of snorty silliness Nev's boys would stamp out.

I interrupted Nev. 'What we need is a guy, or two guys, who will stand at the door and not talk. Just be there, ready to do something if someone gets violent. We don't need help checking IDs or managing the floor. We just need someone who is really big and can handle themselves in a blue.'

Nev spoke again. 'We used to do the Ivy when it was good. We went in there just a year after they had opened and they were having similar problems. We sorted it out …'

By Raffie and Hugh's standards, the Ivy had never been good. Nev's pitch was losing its way. Raffie intervened, 'We want a couple of massive Polynesians. Can you do it?'

'We can do that for you.'

'OK. What's the next step?'

'You fellas look over the PR packs. Then you ring me and let me know how many guys you need for the weekend and on what nights and what times. I'll arrange that and then we'll commence a three-month obligation-free trial period. If at the end of that you decide you're happy, we'll sit down and sign a contract. Remember, you are now accessing a professional, credentialled, reliable agency and anything, I mean anything, you decide you need, or you're not happy with or you want to change, you can just call me.'

He took out his mobile phone and held it in front us as evidence.

'I'm just a phone call away. Call me anytime day or night and I'll take your call.'

We began the trial period that weekend.

Chapter 28
DALE

MY SPIRITS LIFTED. I'D BE BACKED UP BY HUGE MEN, SEVENTEEN-STONE MONSTERS who cast long shadows and scared away anyone I told them to.

The AAA bouncer was due on Friday night at one am. I was excited. Was I about to meet my next teacher? My education as a bouncer would begin again. If there was trouble it would have to go through a wall of Maori. Boom boom boom. I could see him. Face scarred with moku and a wagging haka tongue. He would rub his nose against mine and accept me as his warrior apprentice.

A short fat man approached the rope. 'I'm supposed to be working some place round here, in a lane, some kind of small, raunchy exclusive bar,' he said.

'Are you with AAA?'

'Yeah. This the place?'

Shards of shattered dream fell at my feet.

'I'm Heath. Head upstairs and sign on.'

'Cheers, I'm Dale by the way.'

When he was out of earshot I called Raffie.

'The guy's just shown up … not exactly … no, not a Cook Islander, either … short, fat, white guy red hair, bad teeth … Call Nev! He reckons he's just a phone call away and this guy's not what we asked for.'

Philip came down the stairs.

'There's this guy upstairs. I was thinking, "What's Heath doing letting this guy in?" He starts talking to this woman at the bar, he's all over her and he asked her if she was one of the dancers. You know, "When are you gonna get your kit off, love?" It's funny, but he fuckin' meant it. He thought she was a stripper!'

My phone rang, it was Raffie. Nev would ring us back in half an hour. Just a bleedin' phone call away. I returned to Philip.

'Fat, red hair, bad suit?'

'That's the one. Oh no, it's true! He said he's workin' here. Ohhh, man, you're serious?'

'Sorry, Phil. They promised us an islander.'

'He might be from the Emerald Isle,' Philip joked weakly. 'Didn't we interview for the position? Tell me he's not working upstairs.'

'He's not working upstairs.'

'You know it.'

He went upstairs as Dale lumbered down.

'Phew, wouldn't want to have to do them in a hurry. There's a fair bit of talent up there. The viewing can only get better.'

'You're down here. What did Nev tell you your shift was?'

'Now till close.'

'Sorry, mate. It's just till three am. The owners are a bit tight with shifts. They want to start with an early finish.'

'A two hour shift?! That's a bit rich!'

'If it goes well there's plenty more work next week. This is how we work the door. The patrons line up at the rope. Louise makes the selections. If she lets them in, she opens the rope. If she says no and they ask why, then she'll talk with them for a bit, or not. It's up to her. If they pester her too long, I ask them to move up the fence and continue the conversation with me. Lou turns to the front of the queue and begins again. And so on. If I am having trouble you to step up behind me for effect. Sound alright?'

'So you don't want me to check for ID, or anything?'

'Not tonight. Tonight's a trial. So we'll just take it easy and if you're here again, we'll increase your duties.'

'OK.'

We had planned this approach trusting that the man from the agency would strike terror into the hearts of people still arguing at the fence. Dale was not scary. And he didn't understand what we wanted him to do. He spent his hour talking at women, asking people for ID and interrupting me.

Lou had her back turned at one point and was ignoring two customers we had thrown out the week before. Dale took it upon himself to let them in. I blocked their path.

'Whoa, there, guys. You were thrown out last week, so you ain't comin' in.'

'He just let us in.'

'He wasn't working last week.'

'But he let us in. What are you going to do? Throw us out again?'

Dale grabbed the young guy, from behind and grunted, 'You heard the man, mate' as he threw the guy out by the arse of his tracksuit. I tried to slow Dale down.

'Mate, take it easy we ...'

He was wrestling messily with the second man, young, but bigger than his friend. He had suspicious eyes and wore the same Kangol cap that had set him apart last week. Dale was not faring well. The two of them were on the ground. They rolled out from behind the fence into the laneway. I was staring dumbly at them. Lou was holding the rope and the man in the tracksuit was barking encouragement at his friend like a Jack Russell rounds up a rat.

'Heath, bloody stop them,' Lou said firmly, breaking the spell that held me.

'Oi! Cut it out!'

I bolted out from behind the fence and kicked the capped man in the ribs as he rolled himself up and into a dominant position over Dale. He hadn't seen me coming and as he buckled from the kick, I stepped to the side so that they shielded me from the tracksuit man. I dragged the capped man off Dale and let him fall onto his back, away from me, and Dale jumped to his feet. Instead of retreating behind the rope, Dale looked at the two men and shouted, 'Come on, you little fuckers. You gonna take us both, huh?'

Then he saw that I was not next to him. He saw me and Lou behind the rope and joined us. The two young men taunted us a little, then left. Dale looked at me, incredulously.

'What are you doing, mate? Why weren't you backing me up there? You fuckin' left me hanging.'

'Dale, you started that. You messed that situation up and that's not how we do things here.'

'What do you mean I started it?'

Lou joined in. 'You took the rope and let them in. Then you went straight from talking to violence. They didn't even threaten us and you were all over them like some big and clumsy thing. Shit.'

'Go easy, love. You hadn't even noticed them.'

'I was ignoring them! I knew they were there and I was choosing to ignore them because I knew they had been thrown out last week, because I worked here last week. I know what's going on, and if I want to ignore someone, I bloody well will. I'm going upstairs for a bit.'

'Fuck, what's up her clacker? '

'Dale, I gave you clear instructions and you haven't stuck to them for even fifteen minutes.'

'Mate, you guys run this door like it's a high school reunion. You need some systems.'

'I explained our system and you ignored it. You're not here as an advisor. You're here to do what we tell you to do. It's nearly two. Why don't you sign off now? Grab a knock-off, if you want one.'

'You want me to finish early?'

'Yep.'

'No worries.'

He went upstairs. Pretty soon, I got a call from Nev.

'Good of you to call, mate, he's finishing up ... no, to be honest, he wasn't much good.'

Dale had a point, though. The door did look like a high school reunion. So many of the customers were friends of the owners, or friends of the staff, or friends of friends of the staff. The customers liked that they could chat to security while we were knocking back people in suits. People enjoyed feeling part of something exclusive, particularly the moment when they were let in at the expense of others. They liked Lou's theatricality, as they had Charles's. Lou and Charles did the door as though they were on camera. They hammed it up. They left long stares lingering and they projected their voices. They turned their backs on people with flair and they didn't mind waving off an offensive client with a scathing personal insult.

I could see why the owners put Louise on the door instead of me. My manner was far less dramatic. My tones were lower and I didn't dress outrageously. I didn't have her flair. My job was to be ready when theatricality needed to be replaced by brutality. We needed someone on the door with us who understood the need to let the door bitch perform. Someone with the confidence to leave situations in our hands until they were out of our control. We needed someone who didn't have anything to prove. A humble bouncer. They didn't teach that at bouncer school.

Philip came down the stairs with his arm over Dale's shoulder. Louise was still missing. Philip was explaining, 'It is a strange place, man. It's not like other bars. I know that girl. She's a dear friend of mine, and I know she looks totally wasted, but I tell you in twenty minutes, she'll be tearing holes in the dance floor.'

'She's drunk.'

'Well, she's not exactly drunk, if you know what I mean.'

'No.'

'Look, Dale, it's been great to meet you. I hope we run into each other again soon. I have to get back upstairs now. I'll see you later.'

With a look to me that said a lot, Philip danced back upstairs.

'He's a nice guy, that Philip. Could use a shower, though, and I'm pretty sure he was drinking alcohol up there, on the job.'

'No. He just drinks fruit juice.'

'Do you want me to come in tomorrow?'

'No.'

'What about next Friday?'

'We won't be needing you then, either.'

'Oh. Right then. See ya later.'

'See ya.'

Three hours later it was raining heavily and I was still seething about Dale. I stared at the little electric bar heater, the shabby picket fence that separated the club from the world, the dirty brown fire escape stairs leading up to the dance floor and bar and lounge. I was struck by the squalor of where I spent my work hours, the pools of rain and old piss puddling in the lane, the row of twenty rubbish bins, some festering with month-old food scraps that stood close to where we stood. My anger wasn't just at Dale or Nev. I was angry about standing in the rain alone, protecting other people's good time. I was angry at myself for letting my life lead me to this dark wet shithole of asphalt and compost.

Jogging down the lane in the rain, discernible only by his hat was one of the two men Dale and I had fought with. Stopping hard against the rope, he looked at me and said without a hint of self-consciousness, 'Reckon I can come in now, mate? It's my sister's birthday. No hard feelings about before or nothing.'

'It's been three hours dickhead. Try me in three months. Fuck off.'

'Oohhh, come on, mate, let me in. I've got to see my girlfriend. It's her birthday.'

'So stand there in the rain. You're not coming in here, sister, girlfriend, whatever.'

'You're an arsehole, you know that? A fuckin' arsehole.'

'Piss off.'

'What if I don't? What can you do? What are you gonna do, come out here and bash me? Where's your fat mate? Not so quick to come and have a go now are ya?'

'It's raining and I've got better things to do than beat you again.'

'Come on arsehole. Come out here and have a crack. Throw something, come and get it, come on.'

He looked absurd, sodden and screaming. Why not go home out of the rain, to bed, where I wished I was.

'Unfortunately, mate, you have to throw the first punch.'

To my surprise, he did. I leaned out of the way. As his momentum carried him onto the fence and off-balance, I grabbed him. I dragged him along the palings until we faced each other on the public side of the entry rope.

I kneed him hard, up into his sternum. He softened as the air rushed from his lungs, but he kept punching. He clipped me with some, others missed wildly and some I blocked. The rain was falling hard against us and I could hear the tiny march of its impact over his swearing and the scurries of our feet. As a heavily loaded right went past me, I punched him twice. One into his ribs, one roughly into his kidneys. None of my blows were hard, just blowing off steam, making a point.

He was more committed, screaming that he was going to kill me as he ran at me. He stumbled as I sidestepped but scratched my face as he fell. On the ground and turning around he pushed off hard into me. My forearms caught his shoulders at the height of my hips but he punched me hard in the balls. White shocking pains seared through me and my anger exploded. He pushed me back and quickly straddled himself across my chest. My eyes were wet and squinting with pain, I felt him more than saw him. I wriggled my hands off my groin, out from under his thighs and as I wiped my eyes on a sleeve I saw that his delay in hitting me had been spent reaching an empty bottle. He brought it down hard at me. I drove up with my hips and turned my head away. The glass shattered next to my ear and fragments sprayed cold and nasty against my neck and head.

I opened my eyes. We were inches from the brick wall that was the far side of my laneway. The bin side. The thrust of my hips had thrown him over my left shoulder and I pushed the last of his legs off as I slipped and scrabbled to all fours behind him. While he sought his own crawl I stood over him. I hooked my left arm under his left bicep. My right hand over his right shoulder clenched the far left collar of his track top. As he began to stand I pulled up and in to my chest with my left arm and across his throat with my right. The choke came on immediately.

We sat down together and I asked if he'd had enough. He didn't respond. He struggled a little, but didn't talk. I stopped when all he did was twitch.

I let go of his throat and he rolled away from me like soggy pasta. His head hit the cement with a dull thud and he wasn't breathing. Blood from his head puddled round my shoes – dark, fast-flowing and smooth. Mingling silently with the rain that ran down the lane.

I pulled out my phone and dialled an ambulance. The blood was spreading out over the bitumen. Still no breathing.

'Emergency.'

He sucked in a gurgling breath. I hung up on the ambulance, stepped away from the sodden figure now sitting up and watched it feel the blood running down the back of its neck, pull off its T-shirt and hold it dumbly against its head. Its torso was white, bent and feeble in the soupy nightlight. Looking at it, as the rain coursed over its spine, I thought of maggots. Lost, it found its feet and wavered away on wobbly legs along the lane.

I'll never forget the way his body left my hands – limp and briefly dead. Or the dark solidity of the blood, its unhurried, unstopping flow. The way it spread in all directions, seeking its natural level now that the retaining wall of skin was broken. The guy had started it. He'd asked for something, but not what I'd given him.

Chapter 29

LEE'S ON BOARD

I KNEW LEE WANTED A NEW JOB. HE WAS LIVING AND TRAINING IN THE warehouse but still working at a bottle shop on the other side of the city. He'd been training with Alby and me for a little over three years. With his athleticism and commitment to weight training as well as his experience in marketing and PR, he was perfect. The biggest hurdle was going to be convincing him he could do this job.

When I offered him the job he was keen but baulked at the five hundred dollars it would cost to get himself licenced. The owners knew Lee a little from his visits to the club and his association with me. They agreed he was perfect and put up the money to get him trained. Within a couple of weeks, Lee was at work ready to learn the ropes.

The only downside was that the owners seemed to have stopped chasing Nev for a Samoan. We still received plump and useless iterations of Dale each week who I would politely reject. It was becoming a running joke among the owners. With Lee and Lightning (aka Floyd) on board they seemed to think our security issues had been resolved.

Lee was thrown in the deep end. He started work on a Saturday night. I had fifteen minutes with him and then he was under Philip's smelly and progressively less coherent wing.

'Welcome aboard, mate!' I yelled above the music as Lee and I stood behind the bar signing him on for the first time.

'Thanks. Thanks for hooking this up, mate.'

'No problem. Much rather be working with you than the rough nuts this agency keep sending in. Come on, I'll show you around.'

I introduced Lee to the bar staff and started his tour. It had been a year since Charles had given me my tour.

'Upstairs, which is what you'll be doing for the first while, you get a lot of time to yourself. You know your way around the place and where the toilets are so we won't bother with the full tour. The thing about this job is it all feels pretty cruisy, and mostly it is, nice people to work with. Customers usually just wander around the club enjoying the music, chatting to girls. Most of the time that's what it is, but the moment you hear yourself thinking, "Gee this is cruisy," that's when some prick will take a swing at you just because your back is turned or 'cos you're wearing a number. It is generally a really enjoyable job. Unfortunately, as soon as you start to enjoy it, that's when you are at risk. The knack is to look – and be – relaxed, but never stop looking around, always take note of who's not moving and who's coming and going a lot. They're always the problem – people who are chilled out and happy just wander around the club like well-fed cattle. If someone isn't moving, then maybe lots of people are coming to them or if someone is moving around a lot, maybe coming and going from the club a bit much, they're the ones you need to notice. People who talk to the bar staff a lot or try and be your friend, nine times out of ten they'll be getting thrown out later on. And if bar staff tell you that someone seems nice, make a note of who they are talking about.'

We had settled in together next to the DJ. We were two steps up, looking out across the dance floor. The lay of the speakers created a sort of soundless eddy that made it easier for DJs to make requests of bar staff, or staff to have a conversation.

'Look at it as though it's your lounge room. You're having a party, and basically, you're looking for people disrespecting the place or that need help. You're picking up glasses when you can and checking that people are having a good time. You can't afford to talk to anyone for too long, or something might happen in a part of the house you haven't checked on lately. Does that make sense?'

'Sure. Big lounge room!'

'Yeah. Remember this. If you're going to tell someone to leave, you decide on the reason and no matter what they say, or do, you cannot change your line. If you want someone to stop doing something, then they have to stop. Or go. If you want someone to leave, then they have to leave. Don't ever be drawn into a discussion of your reasons.'

'Why not?'

'Because as soon as you start to talk about your reasons, or think about them, you'll see how petty and subjective they seem, and your resolve will falter.'

'What about really serious stuff?'

'If it's really serious, like a fight, there's no discussion. That's the problem with the job, it switches from being completely subjective and cosmetic to life-threatening and dangerous in a second, and often has nothing to do with what you do or say anyway. You just have to ride it.'

'Great.'

'But don't be scared or put off, it's a buzz most of the time.'

'I'm sure it is. What about the door?'

'When you are down on the door, if you refuse someone, and they turn out to be a friend of the DJ, or they are on the guest list, make eye contact, offer one apology, only one, let them in according to the situation, free or to pay, and don't forget their face or who was with them. People that come with the DJ often think they deserve royal treatment, and if they don't get it their egos get bruised and there's nothing more dangerous than a bruised ego.'

At the end of three months, Lee looked like he'd been there from the day the place opened. He got over his jitters and was even doing the door some nights. He had found an identity for himself upstairs. A kind of homeboy, pit bull, best-friend persona that fitted his physicality perfectly. It kept men on side while making it clear he was an authority figure.

Chapter 30

KNOCKED THE FUCK OUT

ONE NIGHT I HAD COME IN TO THE CLUB AN HOUR AND A HALF LATE. MY TINY little white Honda had been broken into and stolen. It was one am when I arrived. I jogged up the stairs and strode through the bar, signed in, put on a number, grabbed a lemonade and made for the front door. I passed Raffie.

'Sup Raffie. Looks like a good night.'

He leaned hard against the wall, his head tilted back. He had been drinking.

'Hey, Heath. Are you a bit late?'

'Yeah. I called it in. Ran into some car trouble.'

'Right. Look, that's not really on. It's not a good look. Do you understand what I'm saying, mate?'

'If you're saying I shouldn't be late again, I can't promise anything but I'll try, boss. No worries.'

'I'm serious. You're on your first warning if I give you another that will be it, yeah?'

'No worries, mate. It won't happen again.'

'Good.'

I turned to go and under the music and hissed, 'Go fuck yourself.'

I went downstairs and sulked.

A week later, Friday, I was sitting alone at the door, reading. It was late summer and there was plenty of light. Raffie usually showed up at around nine but here he was walking his forward-at-the-hips walk towards me with a white plastic bag of takeaway and a smile. He said, 'Feel like some dumplings?'

'Camy?'

'Of course.'

Camy Shanghai Dumplings. Five dollars fifty for fifteen perfect parcels of pork and pastry. Camy was in a laneway off Lonsdale Street and you couldn't park within a kilometre. The only way to get them to our door was walking four city blocks.

'Sorry about last week.' He looked to see I was getting it. 'Just had a huge line of coke and, you know, just got a little off. Sorry, mate.'

'No worries. I was going to break one of your arms, but we can call it your first warning.'

We laughed. Textbook male bonding. Raffie and I got along. We shared interests in art, taste in music and we'd shared a night of amphetamine madness that ended with tequila shots at eight am. He was volatile, troubled, and would swing from a conspiratorial friendliness making me feel favoured, to being aloof and distant, implying I should not forget my place as his pit bull.

Five hours later it was midnight and the dumplings had worn off. My legs were stiff and the soles of my feet throbbed. Lou was trained up and working as the door bitch, Lee was learning the ropes upstairs with Philip and Raffie was relatively sober.

I went to the office with a tin of takings from the door. I sat down, put my feet up and tucked into a stash of protein bar and soymilk. The desk was a mess of bottles, cups, magazines, publicity offers, overflowing pigeonholes and brimming ashtrays. The computer snoozed beside me and the heating/cooling duct hummed above.

Over the door was the little black and white screen that showed the views of the club's closed-circuit cameras. The screen switched from the door to the bar. From the asphalt where Raffie and Louise paced, silently chatting and smoking, to the mayhem of the bar.

Raffie was talking to someone. The man was taller than him. Lou was skimming into vision on the left side of the screen. Another five seconds of barcam; Raffie still talking. The man was wearing glasses, a dark-skinned South Asian. Five seconds of the bar. Raffie lifted the rope and the guy came in.

I stood up and left the office, crossed paths with the guy as he reached the top of the stairs. Taller than me and paunchy. Perhaps twenty-five years old and coolly dressed. He was at least drunk. Par for the course at one am on a Friday. I went downstairs. The vibe was not good. Lou looked at Raffie. She was unhappy. He shrugged his shoulders.

'I thought he was OK.'

'Which one of us is the door bitch, Raffie?' she exclaimed. 'If you want my job, say so … I told him no and you undermined me!'

A sin. We expected it of Johnny, but not Raffie.

Louise was pissed off, as she often was, and though she was tiny, she could bring down a black cloud like a Marvel Comics mutant.

Raffie and I posted ourselves by the rope while Louise stewed in the stairwell with a grapefruit juice. Raffie defended himself to me, 'It'll be fine. He was fine. Fuck, she'll get over it.'

'Yeah, but you understand why she's shitty?'

'Yeah, but for chrissake, I own the place. If I can't make executive decisions …'

'You pay us to look after the door.'

'I know. I just don't think it's a big deal.'

'It's not, it's one of those little things.'

Forty minutes later Lou was moving about within earshot. Raffie jibed, 'So, Lou, nice hair cut. Who did it, your grandma?'

'Fuck off.'

'No, really. It's a good look. I don't think there's enough of it. Can she do mine? How much does she charge?'

'Fuck off!'

'Could be a nice little earner for her.'

I added, 'You could take a commission, make some extra cash.'

'You two, fuck off.'

The venom was leaving her voice, and in just a minute all would be returned to normal. She came back to the rope and took up her position. Opening the rope and letting patrons out.

'See ya guys, have a good night.'

And letting patrons in.

'Hi, guys, it's a five-dollar cover charge. Have a good night.'

Or not.

'Sorry, guys, we've got a full house. It's members and guest list only. Have a good night.'

The door became busy, with fifteen would-be patrons outside the rope and a stampede coming down the stairs. Lucy, the money girl, processed everyone's cash. Some knew Raffie and wanted to chat. It was a mess, typical of busy nights.

'Are all these people members, then? Huh?'

'Yeah, mate, they are.'

'You people are full of shit. Fuckin' arseholes!'

'Have a good night.'

Raffie was talking to someone who knew his cousin in kindergarten. Louise was juggling two groups of young men. I was trying to speed up the line of payers.

'Guys, can we move to the left and have money ready, please. Five-dollar cover charge. It will really help us if you have the right change.'

I couldn't see Lucy for the people waiting to pay. It was a perfect time for an audacious customer to grab a wad of cash and run upstairs. Lucy was so busy counting money it would be easy to do without her getting a look at the face, and we wouldn't have a hope of finding them upstairs.

A crowd of regulars wanted a word with Raffie and another ten patrons were coming down the stairs. Half of them wanted a pass-out, which made Lucy stop taking money and stamp their hands. Chaos. And I was supposed to keep it all secure.

A guy leaves asking us to remember him.

'We can try, mate, but if it's full there's no guarantee.'

'It's not that full up there, man. You know that. Come on, I'll only be half an hour.'

Fuck off, I thought, but said, 'Look, the numbers say it's full. The management say members only. Give it a shot but I can't promise anything.'

'Duude.'

'Look mate, the more you hassle me, the more likely I am to remember your face and the less likely I'll let you in when you come back, yeah?'

'Cool. Cool. See ya.'

I was looking up towards Lucy. Louise was just in front of me talking to a pair of men. Eight would-be's were still in the queue.

Raffie was a metre away, talking and smoking a cigarette. He was wearing a blue and white soccer top that had been cut up and refigured as fashion. He looked good.

Seven people came down the stairs. I counted them off as I pressed the clicker. Ugly man, pretty woman, blond head, mousey head, dark head with glasses, dark head, blond head. Louise was letting out the first two of the group. Man, dark skin, glasses. I remembered him from the top of the stairs earlier. He bent oddly to his right, clenched a fist and threw everything into a punch. Raffie was facing me and saw nothing. I lunged forward but was never going to get there.

Raffie's head shunted sideways. The cigarette spat out of his mouth and his legs buckled beneath him. I grabbed the guy and we fell into the fence and then to the ground.

Someone was screaming.

The guy was trying to stand up. Hands were trying to shake my grip on his shirt. I held on. If I let go they would be able to run or take a free shot at me. Using him as ballast, I tried to stand as they dragged me along the fence and out into the laneway.

I found my feet and drove into the guy. We fell together again. We were off camera. I was on all fours. My fists gripped his shirt and pushed into his chest. Someone kicked me in the ribs. There were four other pairs of feet around me and everywhere there was screaming. I straddled the guy's chest. More kicks in my ribs.

White light shards and internal noise as something hits my jaw. Holding onto my foe with the inside of my thighs. Punching at his face as I try to protect my head and body. I'm being kicked everywhere. The pain and noise are everywhere. Everything is chaos: sticky tape on my fingers, tearing paper, dropping things, cold spoons on my tongue, shoes that don't fit, the smell of berries, horses' hooves, waking in fright. I'm alone. Lost, battered and blind.

'Hey, bouncer cunt!'

He called before he hit me. I saw him take two running steps. I must have tucked my chin against my shoulder or stiffened my neck. His punch hit the side of my head and knocked me off the dark man, but it didn't knock me out. I wanted it to. I wanted to be gone. Dogs. Little birds. Sleepy.

A second man ran at me and hit me as I raised myself to a crouch. The punch knocked me backwards against glass. The window was frosted and reinforced with wire. Behind it was the money girl's little desk. It didn't break when I smashed against it, but it did when another man punched me. His fist smashed into my face, and my head jolted backwards into the glass. It gave behind me with the sharp crack of weathered wood and I expected to feel my own blood. The world spun and my knees quaked. Comfort, no further to go. The five men were standing in front of me, yelling, but I wasn't bleeding.

Someone was shouting, 'Is that all you've got, ya fat cunt?'

It was me. I was standing up. Remarkable.

Fat Boy replied, 'Come on then, mate.'

I charged and shoved him hard. He fell.

I was berserk with rage. I was ready to kill Fat Boy and his mates, one at a time or all together, but they were picking up their mate and moving away, up the laneway. There was another person there, not attacking me, not attacking them, but shepherding them with his arms, trying to wave the gang up the laneway. The situation was diffusing but someone inside me, insane, kept shouting.

'Where are you going? Is that all you've got! Come on!'

'Heath! Shut up.'

Lou was in front of me, pounding my chest.

'Heath! Heath! Leave it, for Christ's sake. Look at Raffie!'

The crowd of a minute ago had vaporised. Everyone was gone. Raffie was lying where he had fallen – on his back, in that lovely blue and white shirt.

His head was awkwardly propped against his chest where he had slid down the wall and one leg was grotesquely tucked underneath him. His eyes were open and bulging like those of dead fish. His mouth was partly open, and he looked peaceful. He looked far away. He looked dead. Pain started in my head and I don't remember going back inside the rope.

We roused Raffie. Blood soaked his shirt. The skin had been split along his jawbone and the wound gaped open like a wet pair of lips.

My left temple hurt a lot, and so did the back of my head, my ribs and my cheek. Raffie's girlfriend came to see if he was OK and staff came down from upstairs. I thought again how ridiculous it was to be out in the middle of the night, getting attacked by groups of men, for money. What an absurd job.

'You guys have to call an ambulance, or go to hospital. You'll both have concussions. There's no way you can stay here.'

Lou was right, but we did neither. Raffie went home with his girlfriend. I stayed on the door.

At four we were still there, Lou and I. My ribs ached. Both my eyes were starting to swell. I had a raging headache. Lou was tireless and shouldered almost all the work. She was furious with me for staying.

A man leant through the front row of the crowd, and over the fence to get my attention.

'Excuse me.'

'Mate, don't know if you heard but we're full upstairs.'

'Can I just … could you come over here?'

Sore and suspicious I moved a little closer to the fence.

'Don't mean to be rude, it's just that I really want to show my friends the place, they're visiting from out of town.'

'Aren't they all mate? We're flat out.'

He leant further over the fence.

'Do you remember me?'

'No.'

'I helped you before.'

'Whataya mean?'

'Before. In that fight.'

'Oh.'

Lou had overheard. She looked briefly at me mid-negotiation and gave the littlest nod.

'Right. Sorry. Thank you. Come in. Move please.'

I signalled others out of his way.

'Fucking move, out of the way. Thank you. Come in.'

I let him in for free and rang the bar to give him some free drinks.

When the club closed I went upstairs and looked over the video in the office. I rewound the tape to the spot I was looking for. At one forty-eight and thirty-three seconds, the line of people leaving the club came onto the screen. At one forty-eight and thirty-five seconds the recording switched to the bar camera. One interminable second passed. Cut to the door camera and I am being dragged out of the entrance of the club by three men whose faces can't be seen. Raffie's feet are visible.

The camera caught nothing of the incident. It went unrecorded.

I signed off and went home to bed.

Tuesday that week I was training with Lee. We had warmed up and were hitting bags next to each other. I felt light and Lee appeared to rise above me. I woke to him gently patting my face.

'You awake?'

'Yes.'

'Where are you?'

'In the training hall.'

'What's your name?'

'Heath, dickhead.'

'You've been out cold for nearly a minute. I'm taking you to hospital.'

'OK.'

In the hospital bed, under supervision for four hours, I read pamphlets about concussion. Four serious concussions can be enough to cause permanent damage to the brain. I'd had three.

Chapter 31
HERE COMES POLYNESIA

NOW THAT ONE OF THE OWNERS HAD BEEN SERIOUSLY HURT, THERE WAS A NEW urgency in the search for our Maori warrior. My resentment grew as the owners demanded action from Nev after Raffie got pounded. I'd had a gun held in my face but that had been reduced to jokes about the size of the gun.

But for all my disgruntlement, life changed forever the night Oscar walked into it.

I was waiting behind the fence, looking at the absent-minded scribbles and graffiti that had been written on the reverse side by door staff. I was expecting another frustrating despatch from Nev.

'Hey, bro.'

Very quietly a huge Polynesian man had approached the rope and caught me unawares.

'Hey, mate. Are you …'

'I'm Oscar, eh. Here to work.'

'Great. Wow. Come in.'

I felt at ease with Oscar immediately. He was big, at least a hundred and twenty kilos, a little taller than me and he moved easily. He didn't carry his body like a burden. He wasn't obviously muscular. There was a softness about his body and his nature that made him charming and easy to love. But his hands were huge and he could get up the stairs faster than anyone but Lee. Oscar was twenty-six, had three kids and was still playing competitive rugby and basketball. He usually wore basketball boots and track pants but every now and then he turned up in a suit, usually when he was doing back-to-back shifts. His calm physical confidence meant I didn't need to ask any questions about fight training. That and the callouses on his knuckles.

He signed on and came back downstairs. I explained what we needed. Silent, serious back-up instead of the usual zealotry. Oscar simply said, 'So, you just want me to sit here on my stool and watch you and Lou do your thing, and only when some idiot arcs up, you want me to stand behind you?'

'Spot on.'

'Too easy, bro. And if they arc up or something stupid, then I get to slap 'em, eh?'

'That's it.'

'I like it, bro!' Oscar laughed.

And he did just that. I never had to say anything to Oscar about moving away from the rope, or not talking to women on their way in. He was always attentive and at any sign of trouble at the fence he was immediately up and behind me or Lou. He had his stool set up under the main light so that when he stood up from his stool he cast a long forward shadow over me and the person I was dealing with. It had a dramatic effect.

Oscar's assimilation into the security team was seamless. My job was easier, Lou's job was easier and Oscar reckoned it was the cruisiest job he'd ever had.

After about a month, Oscar needed a Saturday night off. He had a gig doing security for the World Wrestling Federation tour. He was going to be one of the big men who chaperone the star 'wrestlers' down the huge steel ramp to the wrestling ring. He was unselfconscious in his love of the 'sport'. When we teased him he giggled and smiled like a kid. He brought a lightness to the job for me. Not just because I didn't have to wear everything nasty by myself, but also because he reminded me that life can be fun, even when you work in a shitty little laneway.

One busy night, Lou had rejected a tall man in a suit. He objected so she had palmed him off to me. Oscar stood up and was behind me but the tall man was unperturbed.

'Yeah, look mate, I'm not saying it's a fair policy but it's the management's privilege to reserve rights. It is up to them.'

'That's why I called you a flunky. Fuckhead. Presumably this is the only job you can get. You look pretty thick to me.'

This went on. He refused to leave and became more and more agitated. Eventually he reached to his right and made a grab for the rope. This is the one thing customers may not ever do. My left hand hooked under his right and redirected his movement in an arc forward of him and up. My arm guided his across my face and I flicked my hand to deliver his right arm sharply against his left hip. He pulled his right hand back and with a quickly clenched fist was about to throw a punch at me with a quickly clenched fist. I may as well have had a month's advance warning and wasn't too concerned. I had plenty of time to think of a couple of different responses when, like the beating of a great black wing, Oscar's right arm swung into view on my right. The suit's punch had barely started moving when the open palm of Oscar's right hand landed on the junction of the right side of his face. The sound was like a thunderclap. His eyes fluttered, Oscar's hand returned to its place behind me and the man folded into the queue of people behind him. He lay on the asphalt for a while, blinking and holding his face before staggering to his feet, staring into the smiling face of my Samoan friend and walking away.

Oscar called after him, 'Suit's a little dirty bro, wanna give yerself a pat down before you try getting in any taxis, eh?'

We persuaded the owners to buy some walkie-talkies and resolved our upstairs/downstairs communication issues. Lee wore one upstairs. Oscar and I wore them too so we all knew where the others were and could call for assistance from anywhere.

With Oscar on board the team, I felt a sense of security I hadn't had since working with Alby and Anefterios. But now I was the coordinator of the team, not the doting apprentice. We were an odd bunch. Lee – short, stocky, stoned and charming. Lou – even shorter, big boobed, big mouthed, volatile and glamorous. Lightning – shuffling and grumpy. Philip – high, charismatic and smelly. Oscar – massive, happy and dangerous. Me – in charge, anxious and increasingly dissatisfied.

The sense of security that came with Oscar was infectious. We saw less and less of the owners at the door. Johnny had pretty much disappeared after the gun. Raffie made token appearances and the rest of us started to develop bad habits. What began as a short sharp shot of tequila, or Strega, at four am to spark us through the last hour became an hourly dose that had our senses softened dangerously by three am. Oscar never participated.

Chapter 32
LONG WEEKENDS

Long weekends and national holidays marked my calendar as a nightclub bouncer the way a steak stands out on a plate. They were big, bloody and always going to take some doing.

If the holiday was on a Monday, it meant an extra night that would be extra busy. On these nights the crowds drank extra alcohol and took extra drugs. Members and DJs supplied extra large guest lists and the owners usually expected us to let in an extra fifty or so people, making sure that everyone paid the extra door charge. Customers would try extra hard to coerce free entry from us.

Extra, extra, extra.

Extra special DJs and additional publicity meant a different crowd. The regulars were still there, dressed to the nines and sporting extra friends. There would be more 'industry' types – music lovers who follow their taste more than the hype. They were out to hear music, not get laid or get wasted.

Dance music purists usually approached the door in little clouds of ganja smoke. They wore designer clothes, discernible from the mainstream by a nip here, a tuck there. Often on the guest list, they didn't crow about it. They quietly mentioned their name or their party and waited. If their name didn't appear, they would accept it with grace and pay the charge – they wanted to hear the music and for them it was worth paying.

As well as these types, the big nights brought other, less discerning clients to the club – muscle-bound outer suburban men, in groups, who came early to ensure entry but complained that the place was empty at eleven o'clock. I was still eating my dinner at eleven!

There were always four or five guys in these groups, usually followed by another group of four or five, fifteen minutes later. Though these groups were savvy enough to split and increase the chance of getting ten men into the club without girlfriends, I could tell from their conversations that it was more a case of two carloads, separated by big night traffic.

Despite the earliness of their arrival, these guys were usually white hot with amphetamines, everyone's breath sweet with the sour sugar smell of bourbon except the designated driver's. The uniformity of their clothes was disappointing – stressed denim jeans, white trainers and faded denim jackets, haircuts from Beckham's back catalogue and clouds of big label cologne.

When the jackets came off upstairs, they would all be wearing tank tops, taut across swollen pectorals. Their deltoids would be huge, body hair absent. By the time the girlfriends arrived, these gangs could number up to thirty. Good for the bar take, bad for the vibe. They swaggered around the bar and sprayed their scent. They were not in the club for the music, the decor or the atmosphere. On these extra special nights, these gangs were here because they'd heard that it was hard to get in, so it must be good, and because of our instructions on special nights, these big groups of men found a way in, when normally they would be stopped at the door.

Even on regular weekends, the three hours before closing time could be unbearable. Everyone developed coping strategies.

We drifted into half sleep, played games on mobile phones, sometimes read books and magazines. Everyone flirted with the money girl.

We ordered drinks all night, every night: apple juice, pink grapefruit juice, Red Bull, coke, lemonade, tea and coffee, gallons of water and stubbies of ginger beer. But when the security guy upstairs heard the request for drinks 'with love' he knew it was a different kind of order. Sometimes they were cocktails from the bar menu in juice glasses. Sometimes they were the creation of the bar man. They looked like a juice, tasted fantastic and two or three would sail you through any pre-dawn, hands-in-pocket, frosty-breath, beany-hat posting.

If the need was serious, really serious, if the person asking for a drink was really struggling, he might ask for a 'soho iced tea': a shot of every white spirit and a little ginger beer. It came to the door spewing frost – murky, dangerous and green. This drink could not be mistaken for juice so it had to be drunk quickly. Its effect was to numb the whole body and make a cold night warm.

Any or all of these strategies might be employed on a long weekend. The extra night and the closing time of seven or eight am brought out the more desperate side in us all.

Exhaustion was inevitable. The hours standing at the door, climbing up and down stairs, listening to entreating stories, throwing patrons out, waking patrons, waiting for them to finish throwing up. You felt as though you were walking through wet cement. Your body pleaded with you to forget about the three extra hours and the little bit of extra pay and quit this fucking job and go home and sleep.

At four am on a Saturday, with a day and a thirteen-hour shift between you and the end of the long weekend, I would watch the stream of clenched jaw, bug-eyed partiers moving around the club, starting their migration to the next venue with a later licence. My mind would drift away from the boucer imperatives – clarity, patience, focus – and join the momentum of the throng. I would step, mentally, into the flow, untie the moorings, take the oars, forget the morning and the noon and night to follow. Sometimes I would seek out the living dead.

Chapter 33

THE LIVING DEAD

THERE HAD BEEN A NUMBER OF 'IN HOUSE' DRUG DEALERS WHO CAME EVERY week and made friends awfully fast. They came and went all night long with endless energy and smiles. Some of them were indiscreet and were given marching orders. Others who had sold a bad batch wisely sought fresh pastures.

'The living dead' came every Friday, Saturday and Sunday night. They weren't always known as 'the living dead'. The name evolved as their physical health declined. At the beginning they were a good-looking duo. In the later stages they were demonic and frightening.

Rick and Maxine worked in marketing and lived together, platonically. They fell in love with the club – the atmosphere, the staff, the crowd, the DJs. They never tired of it. As their attendance continued, their drug use increased. It wasn't long before people were buying from them.

Rick was a gangly Tasmanian who wore work boots and a pimp cloak – all fake fur and impossible colours. He had a big head and mad eyes, even before the drugs took hold. Maxine was a slight blonde, quiet and friendly and, at the beginning, she was attractive.

On the Sunday night of the Labour Day weekend Rick cornered me.

'Australia is a big country, right? Right? Australia has the highest number of golf links per capita in the world and per landmass, and because there is so much desert right, right, there is actually a proportionately smaller habitable land area and so here are all those golf clubs, squeezed together. Where? Here! Right here! You can't spit in Melbourne without hitting a bloody golf course!'

His breath was rancid and he was spraying me as his emphasis increased.

'They're fuckin' everywhere. All the way down the peninsulas and into the Mallee, across to Adelaide and all the fucking way to Sydney! Christ, you could take a year driving to Sydney and play a round every day in a different club, there's just so bloody many. Anyway lots of golf clubs! So what, I hear you say. So fucking what? Well, how many people in Australia? Twenty mill? Let's say four or five million of them are kids or at school and not really going to be playing a whole lot of golf, not yet anyway. Another mill or so are too fucking old to do anything let alone nine or eighteen holes. What a waste of bloody super, I hear you say, and I agree. So what does that leave, nine or ten million? Right now how many people do you know that regularly play golf? Mate, if it's as many as me, it's not bloody many. Look right here. What's in here? Say four hundred?'

'Two hundred here, now. And when it's super, super full it might be three.'

'Right. Right. Lots anyway, or not that many, but a few. Anyway, let's say that two out of ten people in this demographic are partial to a round and that that is a reflection of that remaining ten million nationally. Then you've got two million golf players. Let's add a million to allow for the grey masses so we have three million golf players nationally. Five major cities and with Victoria being one of the more densely populated areas and holding more links per square kilometre than any other fucking part of the country, but not being markedly more populated than the rest of the states per square kilometre. You have to ask, where are all these golf clubs, with their huge properties and low memberships GETTING ALL THEIR FUCKING MONEY FROM?'

This was drug ranting of a high order, but aside from the spitting, it was a harmless way to whittle minutes off the shift.

'Now let's break it down.'

He raved for five more minutes then paused and pulled out a snuff tin. It was full of white powder. He took a tiny scoop from the lid and, in full view of me and the entire club, snorted himself two little caps.

'Want some?'

There I was, three am, four hours to closing, being spat on by a man with a thing about golf courses. For no reason other than I was too tired to muster self-control, I said yes.

I dipped the scoop, blocked a nostril and inhaled. I felt the little pellet of dust hit the top of my nostril and my eyes watered. He snatched back the scoop, put the little kit away and continued his pitch.

'Where was I? Oh, yeah, I was getting a little edgy before, forgive me.'

My pulse rate had tripled, my palms were sweating and my tongue was starting to move independently. I would have forgiven him anything at that moment.

'But my point is that all these golf clubs, if they are going to survive, have to work together. But they won't, they simply will not. So, the future for all these clubs looks particularly bleak from where you and I stand, my friend. This is where me and Maxine come in. We have developed an idea that will unite all the clubs, allow them individual profit gain and virtually print money for Maxine and I. PRINT FUCKING MONEY, MAN!'

'What did you give me?'

'Meth. Good, huh?'

Chrystal meth. I would be awake for at least the next sixteen hours.

'Mmm.'

I was on a ride I couldn't get off. I'd been tired, wasted with exhaustion and desperate for sleep and hot food, but that was a lifetime ago. Now, I was Amphetamine Man, bearer of universal truths. Oceans parted before me and I took whiskey on my weeties.

'So, we are going to … Hey, man, listen …'

Rick held my shoulder and turned me back to face him as I had involuntarily walked towards a packet of cigarettes left on a drink counter. Amphetamine Man only smokes when he needs to, because he is above addiction. I refocused on my mad friend and tried to remember his name.

'We are going to sell them scratchy tickets. Scratchy tickets, man. SCRATCHY FUCKIN' TICKETS! GET IT!'

He was consumed with laughter for the longest time. It bent him over and rolled him on the floor. He convulsed and coughed and lit cigarettes for the two of us and came back to me. He stared into my eyes. He wasn't going to sell anything to anyone. His skin was light blue and his teeth stained a strange yellow-purple. His gums receded dangerously. His head swayed one way, and his body another. He drooled and he stank. I sensed his plan was flawed, but I wanted to believe him so much. Amphetamine Man has unconditional love for all fellow men, especially if they're holding.

Amphetamine Man spent an hour on the door with his work-mates. Oscar and an extra Samoan were down there, seated over the heater, which disappeared behind them, warming a small section of each man's thigh. This was no problem, because Amphetamine Man feels no cold.

The hour turned into two and still I had not stopped talking. Amphetamine Man is always saying something interesting. The Samoans dozed in front of me but I knew they were listening. I'd test them later. With an hour to closing, I went upstairs and found Maxine. She was chatting to someone. The number on my chest broke up the conversation in no time. I took her aside and asked what she was doing later. Amphetamine Man knows no inhibitions.

'We'll probably go to Starlight. Maybe go home first. Wanna come?'

'Yes. Do you have any more drugs?'

'Sure. Now? Or when you finish?'

'Now. What have you got?' Amphetamine Man is a man of action.

Maxine and I took an ecstasy tablet each. I thanked her and said I would like to hang out with her later, but now I had to work. I spent the next hour scouring the floor and couches for drugs. I evicted patrons from couches and overturned their cushions. I banged on cubicle doors and demanded to see the drugs the occupants were carrying. I pushed people out of the way as I crawled over the dance floor. The power of my security number parted crowds before me and lent credence to my scavenging. By the close of trading I had found three different halves of ecstasy and one whole tablet, pink, with an apple emblem on it.

Amphetamine Man collects tax as he sees fit.

Rick and Maxine were stationed in a corner of the bar, watching punters get ushered out of the club. I was blind to the usual duties I should have been performing. Amphetamine Man creates his own job role.

I asked Maxine, 'What are we doing?'

'We thought we would go home first, relax a bit and head to Starlight later.'

'Right, I'll join you. When do we take more drugs?'

Amphetamine Man cannot get too high.

'Well, now, if you like. Have you ever double-dropped?'

'No. Sounds fun. How do we do it?'

Amphetamine Man fears nothing.

'We take two pills at once, and get really fucked up.'

'OK. Let's do it.'

And we did. I've no memory of signing a time sheet that night or of closing the door behind me. I don't know if I had a knock-off drink. I don't know what car I travelled in. I do remember watching the dawn crawl over the ocean as we whizzed along Beach Road. Light stretched up like infants' arms to the blankets of cloud holding the city snug in its shroud of night. I remember the ecstasy catching up to and going past the chrystal meth, winning the battle to control my consciousness. Artificial warmth spread over my body. I could see goose pimples on my arm but inside I was a burning furnace of love and heat.

We reached the apartment. I sat down on the couch. It was morning and someone began to make tea. A man I hadn't seen before and did not recognise was sitting in an armchair wearing a wetsuit on his legs, his chest bare. He was attaching a shade to a light while the globe was on and holding it very close to his face. It made his skin look the colour of packet cheese. Beams of light shone like little suns from his eyes. With the sound of the car gone, and the noise of the club behind me, I was aware of a fluttering in my ears. Tiny wings beat inside my head and the sensation spread as my vision began to blur and shake. The room began to convulse before me, out of focus and fracturing into tessellated planes. I was thinking in screams. Banshee cries flew around my head. I tried to form a word and I think I said, 'How often do you do this?'

I remember Maxine sitting next to me, saying everything was fine, that she knew what I meant and she was feeling the same thing. I remember the man in the armchair moving his mouth and pointing to the light at corners of the room, trying to describe something. The arms of his wetsuit swung round him, slapping against his plastic thighs. Rick fell out of a room to my right with a peal of laughter, pointing at his leg. Blood was running from a gash on his shin. His mouth was moving.

'Ma c uh ha ha ha leeegha wa.'

I didn't know if he was making sounds or saying words. He limped into the little kitchen. Noises came from within. The sounds had shapes and I watched them fly across the room towards me.

More noises came from where Rick had last been. He was fighting with a surfboard, lying on top of it on the floor and howling with laughter. He stood up then and the surfboard grew legs. I panicked, then remembered what an ironing board was.

Normality washed over me. The moment of recognising the ironing board grounded me and for a precious moment I watched with short-lived sobriety as he set up the iron and sipped from a cup of tea. I was in control again. I knew what was happening. I knew it was Monday morning and that this man was getting ready for work. I could read the signs.

I saw that he was in his underwear. His bare legs were twiggy with fine, black hairs, knobbly knees and blood. I began to panic again.

This man. I know him. He's on drugs, like me, and he's going to iron his pants with blood on his legs. Where was he going? He kept laughing and proceeded with his mad task by laying the pants out on the board and releasing clouds of steam that swallowed his head and neck, so he was a decapitated, shrieking, laughing mess working back and forth over the trousers. He pulled the trousers on over his unbandaged leg and did them up. Once on, we saw a wet patch on the crutch of the pants. He saw the patch and was howling with laughter.

'Wha ca e day ah mane e ni li there mar pan I m room ha to go mating a the all hay a roo.'

Maxine whispered, 'He's going to work for a meeting and will be back in two hours.'

My eyes focused. Rick was standing at the door, his hair dishevelled, a cigarette between his lips, eyes hanging from their sockets, scanning the room independently of each other. His shirt was unironed and misbuttoned. His trousers, a tasteful grey, were pristinely ironed on one leg and pathetically crumpled on the other. A wet patch the size of a tea plate over his groin and blood soaking through the ironed leg. His shoes were untied, and he held a briefcase. Maybe it was the briefcase that swayed me. Maybe it was a need for fresh air. Maybe the drugs had fried my brain completely but when he offered me a lift home, I took it.

At every long strip of road Rick would take his hands from the wheel and yell, 'Pipe time!'

I would hold the steering wheel while he took a bong from under the dash, filled it, lit and inhaled deeply. By the time he needed to exhale he would have put away the paraphernalia and taken the wheel. With a deep sigh he would release a cloud of smoke into the car and scream with delight.

As we approached the city I came, at last, to my senses. At a red light I opened the door, stepped out of the car and did not move until I saw a taxi coming. I hailed it, climbed in, recited my address and closed my eyes.

The next week at the club, after days of depression and nausea, when the living dead came strolling to the door I felt sheepish and embarrassed but Maxine was smiling and Rick said buoyantly, 'How bout last week, huh? Blast? Where did you go? Maxine says you came with me in the car, but I don't remember that.'

'I caught a cab.'

Chapter 34
DJ'S LUNCH

A PROMINENT MELBOURNE DJ WAS IN THE CLUB WITH A THRONG MILLING ABOUT him. As the night progressed it was clear that groups were forming. This was a relatively common Saturday night phenomenon, one that officially we disapproved of, but if the group was beautiful, interestingly dressed or particularly good at dancing and drinking a lot of cocktails we welcomed them.

Group-forming occurs when a large group of people meeting for a birthday, a farewell or just a catch up drink, are well versed enough in clubland to arrive in twos or threes, spread over a number of hours.

One was made up of metrosexual homeboys and their girls with fake tits and silly heels. They acted with a studied self-consciousness, like they were trying to pretend that their life wasn't actually that glamorous or amazing.

The other was a group that got very drunk on expensive drinks. They were mostly girls – young, chatty and all over the floor like paint in a pre-school.

One woman was a particularly good dancer. She caught the attention of the DJ. He was predatory and territorial. When other men approached to talk, he held her close. If she stood, he held onto her wrist or clothing and challenged the man who had interfered. He felt he had won her for the night and was protecting his prize. She refused his suggestions that they leave the perch at the edge of the bar and move to one of the cushioned, less populated corners. She shook her head drunkenly while he urged and gestured.

After an hour or so of watching them each time I circled past, I took the opportunity to talk to her while he was elsewhere.

'Where are you lot from?'

'*Phantom of the freaking opera*. We finished tonight. Whoo-hoo. Do you work here?'

'No. I go out wearing a number.'

'Piss off!'

'OK. See ya.'

'No, no. Don't go. Sit down.'

'Oh, no. I think I'd be cutting in on someone. I should walk about. Look busy.'

'Please don't. Stay here, I like the way you feel. I trust you.'

'You hardly know me.'

'Does that matter?'

'This is a nightclub.'

'So? I trust my intuition. When do you finish?'

'Sorry?'

'When do you finish work? I want you to take me home, to my serviced apartment and drink champagne, and tell me about yourself and, maybe, as the sun comes up, you'll fuck me on my balcony, and the cold air will chill the sweat on our skins, and maybe we'll be in love and never be apart again.'

'And maybe I'll be an arsehole and never call.'

'And maybe I have nine forms of hepatitis. I'm willing to take the risk. Besides, I fly out to Brisbane in thirty-six hours.'

'Are you saying this is love at first sight?'

'I'm saying take me home and fuck me.'

'OK, right. I'll need ten minutes to get myself organised.'

'I'll wait, but no more than ten minutes. OK?'

'Yep.'

People presume that this scenario happens to bouncers all the time. It doesn't.

I told Lee what had happened and asked if it would be alright with him if I cut out early.

'No worries! To go home with her mate, you could cut out at the beginning of the night.'

I went to the staff change room and rubbed deodorant in my armpits. I brushed my teeth and checked myself in the mirror. I stopped briefly and considered how different things were at the club for me now, to be able to leave early.

We drove home. She leant across the tiny space of my little Honda's chassis and nibbled at my ears. We found our way to her apartment and stood at the door. Dawn's fingers were just starting their reach at the sky.

'I know I have the key with me. It's in the bag. I'll … just … here it is. Oh, I'm going to have to unpack it. Hold this.'

'Do you want me to look?'

'No. I'll just empty the bag.'

She upended the bag onto the pavement spilling lipsticks, mascara, a wallet, a hairnets, sanitary pads but no key.

'Oh, poo. Here let me … just … I'll call the valet man.'

'Let's pack your bag up first.'

'Oh, good idea. Here. Come here. Kiss me, first, and then the bag and then the man. Mmm.'

We kissed a little, packed her bag and called the valet. She was falling into my arms every few seconds and the valet looked suspicious as I guided her past him.

'Hi, Mr Valet Man. Did you have a good night? We did. Or we are or we … we will, won't we? Would you like to come up for a champagne?'

'No, thank you.'

'No. No. No, of course not. Well, have a good day. Where is the elevator again? Gee, I hope I have my cardkey thing. Bye bye.'

We found the lift and on the way to the third floor she righted herself, stepped away from me, stared and licked her lips.

'What kind of car do you drive?'

'A little white Honda. Remember?'

'Right. Right. This is our floor, are you sure you want to come in?'

'Well, you invited me, it was pretty hard to refuse. I can go if you'd prefer.'

'No, no, come in. You're good, I can tell that.'

She walked directly and unassisted to a door halfway down the hall, stopped, lifted her skirt and from her underwear unhooked a key and a magnetic swipe card. She swiped the card and opened the door.

'Is that key for the main door on the street?'

'Yes. Why?'

'I thought it was lost …'

'Come in.'

She left her skirt up as we entered the apartment and we leant against each other, kissing. We tore clothes from each other and made our way to the bed. She lost her balance, rolled about on the bed searching for me, eyes closed, madly signing, then commanding, 'Where are you? Come here, to me … I said bye, bye Miss American pie … the day the music died … Where are you? Come here. I want you on top of me. Take that off, off. Squeeze me, harder, harder. Lift me up … left, one, two, right, one, two, left one and … ohh, put your finger in me. There, there, there.'

'Are you OK? Hey, look at me. HEY!'

She looked directly at me, out of a dream, sharp and present. Her left hand gently gripped the wrist of my right hand. A moment ago it had driven my fingers further and further into her, now it stayed me, warily.

'I, I don't think I want to fuck you. I think I just want you to kiss me and hold me. I'm not sure how much I want …'

I removed my hand. 'Do you want a drink? I'll get you some water.'

'No, no, there's champagne in the fridge. Get that.'

'You're sure?'

'Yeah, it'll be nice.'

I went to the kitchen and got two glasses and a bottle of champagne from the fridge. I was feeling increasingly uneasy about the situation. This was a male fantasy alright – a beautiful woman, naked in the next room, wanting to drink champagne with me, and a minute ago wanting me to ravage her. However, my instincts told me not that she was there for the taking but that she was in trouble.

Back in the bedroom she was writhing on the bed clutching her crutch and thrusting it into the air. She was squeezing hard at her breasts and licking her lips ferociously.

'Peggy Sue … oooh ... ooh … Peggy Sue. I love you. Where are you? Come and fuck me. Get it out. I want you. Put that down. Hold me, squeeze me, please, fuck me, I want you inside me.'

She rolled to the edge of the bed, undoing my pants and stroking hard against my crutch. She grabbed the top of my jeans and shook them as if to pull them away from me. And I stopped her.

'Hey, look at me, hey …'

I realised with a shock that I didn't know her name.

'Look at me. Listen to me. Can you hear me? I want fucking. I want fucking. Come on, fuck me, fuck me, don't be shy, get it out and put it in. I'm ready, now, now, now.'

She was on all fours, pointing her vagina at me, toying with it and thrashing her head about. Sun was breaking through the Venetian blinds and I could hear cars going past in the street outside. I walked around the bed.

'I'm not going to fuck you. What have you had tonight? Is it just alcohol?'

She looked at me. Her pupils were dishes, swimming in her skull. Her mouth and lips running with saliva.

'Oohhh, please, I just want to make love all night. Now, please.'

She rolled onto her back and continued her pornographic dance.

'I'm going to leave, but I'm worried about you. I'm not sure I should leave you like this. Can you hear me?'

She couldn't locate my voice. She looked at different points in the room while begging for sex and playing with herself. She was directing her voice to me but couldn't see me. She was beautiful. Her body was lithe and ripe. The muscles bulged impressively under the skin as she lifted herself off the bed and rolled about.

'Did you hear me? I'm going to leave. I just need you to tell me that you're going to be OK.'

I wasn't waiting for her to tell me she was alright. I wanted her to tell me she understood that I'd not meant to take advantage of her.

'I hope you're OK. I didn't know you were so wasted. If I'd known I would have just left you at the door. Listen to me.'

Whatever she was on seemed to be getting stronger. Her focus was gone from her genitals. She was sliding round the bed, stroking her face, running her fingernails along her stomach. Her eyes were shut and she was mumbling about the importance of sunlight in the life of a dancer. I got a clean sheet from the wardrobe, threw it over her and left.

Chapter 35

BIG HAIR

I was at the door facing down the tallest women in Melbourne. It was Melbourne Fashion Week. The club was hosting an event. I was holding the door list. On it were the names of modelling agencies with plus-ten and plus-twenty next to them. If someone said the name of an agency, I let that person in and subtracted one from the list.

The models had skin that looked plastic and delicious at the same time. Their hair was ruffled like they'd just fucked and their clothes were barely there. Most had uniform breasts and legs that were more than half their body height. I was shorter than all of them and taller than the men that buzzed around them. For the first hour I was mesmerised. *Vogue* and *Harpers* had come to life.

She was six-three easy without heels and maybe six-six with. Her skin was dark chocolate and swallowed the light around her. She was wearing a loud, rainbow-striped dress. Her hair was a bouncing Afro. She was gobsmackingly, amazingly beautiful. I could see nothing but her.

'Good evening.' A train of attendants hustled to a halt behind her. She smiled, lighting up the night.

'Open the rope.' Her voice was honey.

'Aaaah … aaaah … are you …'

'Am I what?'.

'Are you on the guest list?'

'I'm here.'

'OK. Yes. But I need to know what agency you're with.'

Her voice changed and she commanded, 'Open the rope.'

I may have been dazzled and drooling, but no one talked to the door bitch like that.

'Are you on the guest list?'

'Does it matter? You want me in your club, don't you?'

'Only if you are on the guest list.'

The members of her party looked at each other in disbelief. She raised herself high on her heels and looked down at me.

'Open the rope, little man.'

'Excuse me?'

'I said, let me in little man.'

'Sorry love. If you don't tell me your name, I won't know if you are on the list.'

'You stupid little prick. I'm leaving.'

'See ya.'

It should have ended there, but her group didn't want to leave. They clustered round her and cajoled her back. A man in a fine suit and chunky spectacles stepped out from behind her.

'We're with Perfection. I'm Richard Stiggley.'

The name was on the list.

'There we are. "Hey, presto", the door flings wide. Come on in, folks, and have a great night.'

Her eyes bore into me as she glided past.

Two hours later I took a break from the door. Philip came downstairs and I went up to have a look. Empty champagne flutes stood everywhere. Beautiful people danced in beautiful clothes. I felt runty.

It was difficult, with the lights and her skin to see her face, but her height and her hair stood out everywhere. Whether she was dancing or at the bar, everybody was looking at her. She knew it and enjoyed it. Patrons, especially males, stepped aside in awe, or fear.

Because she was, apparently, someone, we were told to make her comfortable, which meant doing the things she asked, but we didn't throw anyone out for her.

She was given drinks, and sat with the owners, laughing conspicuously. When her lioness strut stirred the unwanted attention of inebriated men she demanded they be removed from her sight. It wasn't long before the walkie-talkies ran hot with our loathsome observations of her prima donna antics.

Hours later, in the hazy part of the night when people started to look ragged, and the music had tightened its grip, I was moving towards the toilets and right in the middle of the passage, clearly lit by footlights, lay a great pile of vomit. It steamed, lit hideously by the footlights.

The pile was no drug adjustment puke. It was a whole bowl of pasta, bread, salad and mixed drinks. I stepped around the spreading mire, and told a bussie to get buckets of hot water and a load of tea towels.

I stopped a couple racing towards me and warned them of the spew. They thanked me and moved carefully through the passage. Patrons were coming towards me from the other end, returning from the toilets.

I called, 'Guys! Watch out, don't stand in this.'

'Eeeee.'

'Oooo.'

'Look out.'

'Aaaa. That's fuckin' rank.'

'No shit. Whoa, careful walking through here, there's …'

'Nngghh.'

'Yeah, vomit. Just be careful. STOP! Look down. Yeah, yeah. It's gross.'

The patrons were getting harder to manage. Despite their revulsion they were lingering and staring, blocking traffic. I was able to warn them as they came from my end of the corridor, but the other end was a problem.

Just as I was thinking I should move to the other end and clear people out, I heard her voice.

'I'm going to the toilet and then I'm coming back and you, my dear man, are going to buy me a drink, so you just wait here. I said, WAIT HERE.'

She appeared beside me, six feet tall and more, looming over me with her hair and chiselled features, her catwalk legs and skyscraper heels.

'Don't go through there, there's …'

'Out of my way.'

'No. Listen. Don't. There's …'

She pushed me out of the way.

'No one. No fuckin' body tells me what or where the fuck to go, not you or not any …'

And yep, she slipped in the spew. Both legs flew out in front. She fell into the vomit, her lower back hitting the ground first with a satisfying plop. Her head was jolted backwards and thudded into the floor. Her hair picked up an assortment of biley bits and she screamed. Her fall would have hurt a short person, but she was very tall and the way she went down, it couldn't have hurt much more.

I stepped into the corridor, and offered her my hand.

'Fuck off just fuck off you prick fuck off fuck fuck fuck fuck off.'

She ignored me and tried to stand up alone. She put both hands on the ground but they slipped in the spew and she lurched forward and lay face down in it. Her screams doubled in intensity and volume. Her hair, which revealed itself to be a wig, fell off her head and lay like an oversize steelo pad, soaking up grizzly bits from the floor. Now she took my hand, the fluids and food pieces squelching between our palms as she gripped and stood up.

'You fucking cunt you cunt you cunt cunt cunt. This is the end you little, little cunt of a man. I hate you, do you hear me?'

Her dress was dripping with vomit. Pieces of half digested food fell from her clothes, her arms and her face. The skullcap that held down her real hair down was slick with someone else's bile. She shook with rage. Guttural noises belched out of her. She stepped gingerly through the stinking mess, collecting her vomit-coated handbag on the way. Her aide escorted her to the toilet and she could be heard swearing from the sink where she tried to repair herself.

I collected a rubbish bag from behind the bar. I put the big, wet wig in the bag and went to the women's toilet. She was still at the sink.

'Shall I leave it here for you or would you like me to just put it in the bin?'

I didn't stay to hear her abuse.

Hours later I was at the door in the cold, drinking a cup of hot tea. I held the cup close to my face and the steam rose to warm the air as it entered my nostrils. I was lost in this little sensory grace when Rachel and a friend approached me from the club side of the fence. They both looked tired. It was four-thirty am. Rachel was as cute as ever with her black bobbed hair and white skin. Her eyes were a dangerous jade green, even in the dark. Her friend was a little taller, blonde and graceful. She looked about shyly. I lowered my cup.

'Hey, Rach. Didn't see you come in.'

'Hey, we had a really good night, but I just really wanted to tell you that we think you're a prick.'

'Yeah?'

'Yeah.'

'You're a fucking arsehole, the way you laughed at that poor woman.'

'What poor woman was that Rachel? Are you going to introduce me to your friend?'

'Bec, Heath, Heath, Bec. The way you laughed at that model. It was so cold-blooded. You were so nice once ...'

'I seem to remember that that was my 'big problem', Rach.'

This brought a smile to Oscar who was lounging on a stool in the shadows. Rachel seemed genuinely upset.

'The poor woman who fell over in the spew.'

'Oh. That woman. I hope she swallowed some.'

Oscar let out his girly giggle.

'That's just fuckin' rude.'

'See you next time, Rach, unless you're never coming back.'

She didn't reply. They walked up the lane and I put the cup back under my nose. The steam wet my whiskers and I was lost again.

To Rachel I had become a prick. There was no point explaining to her how the woman had behaved. How she had been rude, and that she had snubbed my advice not to walk. Rachel hadn't seen her prancing about the bar all night as though she owned it, and Rachel didn't hear the things people call me on the door all night, every night. Sometimes it's easier to just give people what they want. If they want a bouncer in their Saturday night story to be a prick, so be it.

My phone rang the next Monday and it was Rachel.

'Hey Rach, calling to give me another serve?'

'No. My friend the other night, remember her? Her name is Bec.'

'Yeah, I guess so. I was a little distracted by the lady and the spew.'

'Shut up. Despite my warnings, Bec wants me to tell you to call her, or could she call you? I told her what an arsehole you are, but she still seems keen. So there it is. Want her number?'

'Sure. It's obviously going to piss you off.'

'Arsehole.'

I took Bec's number and called her. We arranged to meet. She hated nightclubs so the only real way for us to get together was during a lunch break when she was at work. She worked at a gallery in the city. Tuesday week. Two weekends away. Before that date was the club's third birthday. Lee, Philip and I had all agreed that we would let our hair down together for this night. It was invitation only so it would be super-busy but pretty safe.

Chapter 36
ANNIVERSARY

PHILIP WAS UNHAPPY ABOUT THE CLUB. HE COMPLAINED THAT IT DIDN'T FEEL as safe as it used to. It was true. The crowd had changed. There were fewer designers and intellectuals coming through the door. People were coming from a broader cross-section of the community and with that came new tensions. There was more speed around and with it aggression. Younger patrons were coming and drinking excessively. We had ugly nights where nothing too bad happened, no fights or concussions but by the time we shut the door we were all exhausted. Manhandling drunks, listening to crap on the door, explaining that we didn't do twenty-firsts, finding the guy that was groping on the dance floor – it was tiring.

None of this would be a problem for the birthday night. All the old regulars would come out of the woodwork and it would be just like the old days.

The Friday passed without a remarkable incident. Three or four people were ejected from the club in Oscar's shadow. I spent about ninety minutes listening to abuse at the door. No big deal.

Lee and I trained on Saturday morning. We wandered up to Smith Street and ate breakfast from a Vietnamese bakery. We worked, trained and lived together. We saw more of each other than most couples and a lot of the time we spent in each other's company was watching that the other was safe or trying land a punch somewhere on his body. We didn't talk much about how we felt. When you spend so much time hitting each other or backing the other up physically, the usual wrinkles of a friendship get ironed out pretty quick.

I went off to work at six thirty to start at seven. Lee normally started at ten but on this special occasion he was starting at eight. The owners had invited four hundred people. Two seventy and the place was heaving.

By midnight there were three hundred upstairs. The door was easy. If they didn't have an invite or a pass-out they couldn't come in. We didn't see the owners for hours, they were busy upstairs. Philip arrived in a pink and purple outfit of chenille and sequins. His belly hair looked fantastic, groomed, and even the abscess on his cheek looked like it had been daubed with foundation.

Oscar wore a version of a suit. Black pants, dinner jacket and a T-shirt printed with a shirt front and cravat. His hair stood out more electrically than normal and an Afro comb stuck out from the top of his crop. Lou looked incredible. Cowboy boots polished to a high gloss. Fishnets, miniskirt and a tight black singlet. Her ample bosom sat proudly and her lipstick was as shiny as her boots. Lightning wasn't dressed up at all. I still wore all black but my shirt had a collar and Lee's T-shirt was new.

At one thirty people were leaving because it was too crowded. A regular came downstairs. A big guy that worked in hospitality, he often playwrestled with Lee and I. Tonight, rather than feigning a punch, he handed me a little plastic bag full of pills. He stared into my eyes and was very far away.

He walked out into the lane and said as he left, 'Tough cunts like you lot can probably hack them. I'm fucked.'

I saw Lee look at my now-closed hand, then at me. We looked at each other. It was silly. Irresponsible. But at two-thirty Lee and I swallowed a pill each. Lou had one and Lightning took two, saying he would catch up later.

Half an hour later we were leaning against the wall by the rope. Lou had declared herself unfit to work and gone upstairs. Oscar was doing all the talking because Lee and I simply couldn't. Neither of us could move our legs. We had locked our knees and were concentrating on keeping our eyes from rolling back in our heads.

'Why don't you boys go upstairs? I'll handle the door,' Oscar said at three-thirty.

It was completely against policy but so was recreational drug use. We never normally used the goods lift, but we weren't going to get up the stairs in our condition. The lift opened into the club's storeroom. The door from the storeroom into the corridor of the club was ajar. The storeroom was thick with smoke and a circle of people – some employees and some not – were sitting in a circle smoking joints, snorting lines, drinking and chatting. Lee fell face first into the circle and I fell over laughing. We crawled out of the storeroom and continued through the club. There were legs everywhere. Where was Lee?

'Lee, wait for me.'

'I'm behind you.'

He was. We drew level and crawled on. Legs everywhere. Voices saying things, laughing, squealing, 'What are you clowns doing?'

Someone shunts us sideways. Lee punches them in the nuts. They grab him, see his number and let go. He falls back onto all fours and we laugh. Keep crawling into the bar. The music is louder than anything ever and there are too many legs. We crawl together and sit down. A cigarette comes from somewhere. I can't hold it properly. The smoke makes my mouth feel hollow and sandy. I try to bite. My tongue bleeds. Now I'm tasting the smoke.

'Lee, I'm eating the smoke.'

He is lying down.

'We should move.' I tug at his pants.

He sits bolt upright and stares hard into me. 'I gotta place some bets.'

'What? Bets?'

He's adamant. He stands and so do I. I follow him and then we are hugging with Philip and I can smell his acid sweat. We are all moaning love for one another. I'm gagging. There's still blood in my mouth. Something splashes on all of us. There is a hint of nausea. Lee's still looking for a bookie to place his bets. Something hard hits my head and Lee looks for something that has hit him. A barman is throwing ice at us.

'Wanna gillim,' slurs Lee. We trundle together to the bar and start wrestling the barman. The floor is sticky and my face is stuck to it. I cough. Alby's voice is in my head. 'Cunts like that are just askin' to get bashed.'

Now I'm looking out the windows at the back, out into the night. Lee is next to me again.

'Feel ... incredible, like my arms are wings.'

'Me too. Yeah need drink. My eyes are sweaty.'

'Let's find Philip.'

Moving through the bar it seems quiet. Lights are on.

'Done taking in the view, boys?' It's Oscar.

'Time?' we chime.

'Quarter to six.'

I look at Lee. He looks like I feel. Surprised and terrified. Hours have been lost.

'Philip?'

'Gone. Said he'd see you at Starlight.'

Lee and I make our way out. The sun is coming up. Sunday morning in the city. The steam and squeal of street cleaners. Occasional calamitous crashes of empty beer bottles tipped into a bin. Taxis trawling for fares. Hungry-faced people and that blasting city wind. My jaw is cramping and I taste vomit. Lee and I walk past the quiet theatres, ornate and quivering with the effect of the drugs. We are covered in sticky half dry goo, from the bar floor. We stop in a 7-Eleven but the light is corrosive and we leave without purchase. Into the Exhibition Gardens. The trees are so tall we both have vertigo and need to lean on each other.

'You do the forward motion and I'll do the directions,' Lee says. It works. We lean hard into each other. I focus on forward momentum. The trees breathe and sway at me. I love them. I'm not cold anymore. The wind has stopped. The trees are my friends. I feel connected to Lee and to my workmates and to my job and to my training and to the trees. I'm not worried. The knot that lives in my stomach is gone.

I notice it by its absence. Except for when I'm training, fighting or high, I am anxious – hunted.

'How you doing?' I ask Lee.

'Wondering what happened, wondering what we took?'

'Me too.'

We keep up our tandem stagger through the park, past the dry fountain and the marble gods with their serpents and gestures.

My phone rings. I find it and answer.

'Hello.'

'Heath?'

'Yep'

'It's Lou.'

'Yup?'

'Did you hear about Philip?'

'No, what? Last I saw him, I think we were wrestling in the bar.'

'He went to Starlight. Some guys saw him in that outfit and bashed him. Really badly. He's in hospital.'

'Where?'

'Vinnie's.'

Cunts like that are just asking to get bashed. But they're not. Philip just wanted to have a good time.

'Lee, gotta turn hard right.'

'Why?'

'Philip's in Vinnies. Bashed, hard right!'

In our muddled way we helped each other up to the hospital a block away. The hospital security saw us coming and told us to go home unless we needed to see a doctor. We said we did but couldn't see straight or hold a pen to fill in the forms. They said they didn't know who Philip was and we eventually leant against each other and manouevred our way back to the warehouse.

Philip suffered three broken ribs and serious concussion. A broken nose, two teeth gone, a broken cheekbone and some guy's boot had ruptured his anus. When I did eventually see him, pink, purple and bandaged against the hospital linen, under harsh lights, all I could think was that he looked like I felt. I sat next to the bed and held his hand.

Through his swollen gums and purple lips he said, 'All vith twaining oo do. Wha id fuh?'

'So I won't be afraid.'

'Oo there et?'

'No.'

I was always afraid. I couldn't look at a person without assessing what risk they might be to me. I struggled to form friendships because my suspicion was so engrained I repelled people. Philip was light where I was dark. He trusted everyone, he wanted everyone to be his friend and come in to the club and everything would be fine. The club needed both of us in equal measure but I was worn out.

Philip was worn out too. He'd been going balls to the wall for over two years. Two years of not sleeping from Friday morning until midday Monday. He was an icon, briefly, of the Melbourne clubland. But the nights of snorting powder off toilet and table tops, the casual sex, dancing through the wee hours and not eating four days a week were taking their toll. The weeping abscess on his cheek that hadn't healed in four months. It fluctuated in size and wetness in tandem with his sleeplessness. His hair was grey. He smelt bad all the time. He was attached to a loud, abrasive and unhealthy looking Irish stripper who demanded he party harder and longer than ever before. His Ford had broken down in Cheltenham and been left to rot. He needed a rest.

Chapter 37

REALLY SPECIAL GUEST

'Hey, mate, how are you?' Two men approached the rope.

'Evening, guys. I'm alright.'

'Hear you stole my mate's lunch a few weeks back.'

'Eh?'

'You know, stole his lunch. He reckons it was cut and ready to take to school.'

'Don't know what you mean.'

'Bullshit, mate …'

It was the celebrity DJ who had been in the club when I left early with the girl from the *Phantom of the Opera* musical.

'The dancer. I was fuckin' home and hosed and you took her out from under me, mate.'

'Oh, right. Yeah.'

'Yeahhh!'

'I took her home and left her there. Nothing happened.'

'I find that pretty hard to believe.'

'That's up to you, mate. Think what you want.'

'Mate, she was fine and she was so dosed up, I reckon by the time you got her to your car she'd have tried to ride the gear stick and unless you're a poof you would have had a turn at her.'

'You sound pretty sure of all that.'

'I fuckin' should be. Cost me enough getting her there.'

'Don't flatter yourself, mate. It was more than a few drinks she had in her.'

'Don't I know it.'

'What?'

'The shit she was on doesn't come cheap.'

'If you want to boast about your 'Class A' credentials, do it somewhere else, around someone who gives a shit.'

'Mate, I'm not talking about Class A's. The shit I give her is a lot harder to come by.'

'Eh?'

'I reckon you probably said enough, mate. Let's get go in,' his friend said.

'Nah, I've got a point to make. She woulda fucked all night, anyone and anything, and he cashed in on it.'

'I didn't touch her, buddy, and by the sounds of it, it's a good thing I took her home.'

'We're leaving, now,' his friend said.

'Good,' I answered.

'Bullshit we're leavin'. I'm going up here for a drink,' said the DJ.

'I don't think that's such a good idea,' his mate said.

'Neither do I,' I agreed.

'Well I fuckin' do. You don't let me in I'll call one of your employers and have them come down and let me in mate, so open up your little rope and let me the fuck in.'

I felt Oscar move behind me but stayed him gently with my right hand. There was no way to avoid letting this guy in. He was close to the owners, all of whom were upstairs. I had no proof of what he had done and keeping him out would be messy. It might have been easier with Lou there but she was upstairs. I felt sick and angry and dirty. I lifted the rope and he and his friend entered.

'What happened there, bro?' asked Oscar.

'Remember that girl I left early with a couple of weeks ago?'

'Yeah. You fuck her?'

'No. It got really weird and I left her at her place. Got really weird.'

We sat in silence.

Images of that young woman had haunted me. The wildness in her eyes. The foam at the corners of her mouth. Her body writhing like something possessed on her hotel bed. All this training, all this responsibility, all this respect I thought I had earned was worth nothing in the face of a little celebrity. The way the woman had tapped into my own base needs and the way I felt I had compromised her, even though I didn't do anything, made me angrier and angrier. I felt like an unwilling participant in this man's crime, and powerless to extricate myself from it.

'Can I come in?'

'No.'

'Dude, come on.'

'Dude, no.'

'Dude if you're not gonna lemme in I'm just going to stand here until my friends come out.'

'OK.'

'Even if that's like two hours?'

'Nothing I can do to stop you.'

'Alright, guess I'll just stand here.'

'OK.'

'OK.'

'OK.'

'You know what the greatest predator in Africa is? I'll tell you … it's an ant man, an ant that the farmers of the massai call siafu …'

'Right, just step out of the way of the rope, please. I need to let these people in, thanks. Hey guys.'

The little guy continued. 'It's not lions or tigers or even hippos. This ant, that lives in colonies of twenty million. Twenty million, man. That's an ant colony with more ants than there are people in Australia. When they're on the hunt they can kill anywhere up to a million living creatures in a day and the farmers, what do you reckon the farmers do?'

'Farm?'

'Seriously dude, the farmers, they don't do anything because the ants are usually only eating scorpions, beetles, stuff like that, stuff that would otherwise be eating crops, even rats and mice. The ants are like a natural pesticide, score one for permaculture. But, but. Listen, but …'

'But you're in the way. Just move back up the fence here away from the rope.'

'Are you interested man? This stuff will blow you away.'

'Riveted.'

'Right. Anyway, like I said, most of the time this ant is sort of benign, on a human level but if livestock are tied to a pole and unattended and the ants come across it and the farmer isn't there to like get them off, its goodbye little goat or whatever. They fucking eat whole chickens in like four days. But get this, the way larger animals die, including sick, drunk or infirm humans and babies – bear with me – and babies, is by suffocation. The big ones bite a hole and the little ones follow in and make the hole bigger and so on and so on. Ants all over the body, in the windpipe, the victim fucking suffocates. How's that, how's fucking that!'

'Wow. Move up again mate, you're drifting into my workspace. Come on in guys. Feel free to listen if you wish or there's a nightclub upstairs for a five-dollar cover charge. Thought so, just pay the lady, cheers.'

'You know you can't stop me standing here in front of the rope.'

'You can stand there if you want but if you interfere with me being able to do my job then it's over to my Samoan friend here.'

'Alright, so on with the siafu.'

'Mmm.'

'If the farmers see the siafu they know it will be a good year but they also know they will have to be vigilant. And get this, man, they – scientists and shit – know how they communicate, sort of, they know at least that they communicate through chemical messages, scents or vibrations left by each ant dragging their abdomen on the ground, except for the carrier ants in the colony who are always carrying the pupae of a sister, 'cos all the ants in the colony are women, yeah, it's this total fucking sisterhood. Not a conspiracy theory man but don't tell the witches, so when they stop to rest and hatch their young which, while they're on the move, they do every four days, at which time the carriers will clean, stack and maintain their pupae until it hatches and they replace it with another that they'll carry to the next destination. All of this is communicated to all the ants that are involved in guarding and organising the new nest. This is like the whole of Australia setting up camp on Uluru and being totally organised, no one arguing, no one being a prick at the door and everyone getting fed, 'cos that's why the ants kill so much shit man, to feed themselves. It's not for sport, yeah like all of Australia camping at Ayers Rock blah blah but communicating only through smell and dragging their arses on the floor.'

'You getting all this, Os?'

'Every word.'

'I shit you not fellas, every word I speak is true. Wait man, the most amazing part is coming up.'

'The bit about what if we could all get along like this and why don't I let you in?'

'No, no. Reproduction dude. How do they reproduce if they're all female?'

'Turkey basters?'

'Hah hah. Ever heard of a sausage fly?' the little guy asked edgily.

A small group approached the fence.

'No, do you know anything about sausage flies guys? Good, if you did, I would not have been able to let you in. Enjoy. Stay there, Professor Bellamy. Aren't you just getting to the good bit?'

'Alright, alright, sausage flies are like ten times the size of the largest siafu ants, the ones with the big teeth, these sausage flies are shithouse fliers and they have this big sausage-like sack attached to the back of them and for some reason they tend to wander into the colony while it's on the move. Fuck knows! When they do this the siafu pounce on them, control them, cut off their wings, and often cut off their heads but they don't kill them. Why? Because the sausage fly is actually the male of the species! It's fucking incredible. There is enough sperm in the sack of a sausage fly to inseminate fifty million siafu mothers. That's like you or me fucking every woman in America and Canada and probably Venezuela and they all have babies and all the babies are girls.'

'Where does the sausage fly come from?'

'That is a very good question! So they take the sausage fly without his wings and head and bundle him off to the lair and have their way with him and he is the only creature that crosses their path that they don't try and kill on sight.'

'That your phone?' The little guy's focus was broken.

'Oh. Yeah. Hello. Yeah, man, it's me. I'm stuck outside. This shit is incredible. I've just been talking fucking shit a thousand miles an hour for like twenty minutes. They won't let me in. Come down. You're fucking where? Oh, for fuck's sake, that's like a twenty-dollar cab ride man. Come and meet me here. It'll be much better, what? Nah man, he'll let us in. We're getting along good. Will you let me and some mates in?'

'No.'

'Alright, fuck it man, I'm on my way. Without a look the little guy turned and charged away, up the lane.

'See ya,' Oscar and I called after him.

'Heath, you there mate?' Lee's voice came through in my little earpiece.

'Yeah Lee, what's up?'

'You want to come up here. Some guy's up here mouthing off to the owners. Thought you might want to hear what he's saying. He's by the bar.'

'Cheers.'

Lou had come back downstairs. I muttered at her I was going upstairs. Oscar had heard in his earpiece and looked at me with reassurance. I took the stairs four at a time. I found my DJ mate standing in the middle of the bar with all three owners. Lee was off to one side. I joined him.

'What's he saying?'

'Telling the guys you gave him a hard time at the door.'

I should have stayed away. The owners knew me. Anything he said would be taken with a grain of salt. I stood next to Hugh and made eye contact with the DJ.

'Here's the prick now!' he exclaimed.

The owners turned to look at me.

'Guys. Everything alright?'

'Well. Our mate here was telling us the two of you had a disagreement at the door,' Hugh said with a question in his eyes.

'We did. It was over the civil rights of women in night clubs and whether or not they deserve to expect their drinks to remain untouched,' I said.

'What?' Hugh asked.

'This guy's full of shit. He was just being a prick not letting me in,' the DJ said.

The owners looked at me. I said to the DJ, 'Time for you to go.'

'Time for you to get fucked,' the DJ laughed at me.

'You gotta go, mate.'

'What?'

'You're out.'

'Fuck off. You can't throw me out. You'll lose your job.'

'Be worth the job to change the way you look. You walking?'

'I'll be calling you guys on Monday, get rid of this cocksucker, or you don't get any more of my acts.'

He walked in front of me through the carpeted corridor and into the chill-out area. The owners were clearly confused. They were also high and probably enjoying the theatre of the scene.

Before heading down the corridor towards the stairs and the street he turned around.

'There was nothing in that bitch's drink mate, she just wanted to fuck me 'cos I'm a big DJ. Whole lot more reason than you give the ladies.'

'Keep walking.'

Along the corridor, down the first flight of brown wooden stairs. And the second. On the landing at the third and final flight before ground level and the doorway to the laneway he turned to face me. Not yet in view of Oscar or Lou, he smiled and screamed, 'No, no! Don't push me. NOOOO!'

He threw himself head first backwards down the stairs and fell in a heap on the lower landing.

'Oh, God, my back! You fucking cunt. I'm gonna sue you, cunt. They all saw it, you cruel, fucking cunt. My back. Oh God, my back,' he screamed.

The two or three customers waiting to get in had seen a man fly backwards down the stairs, apparently pushed by me – the bouncer. Oscar was coming along the fence to remove the DJ who had stood up. I should have let Oscar eject him. I moved down the stairs and signalled Oscar to stand back. I approached the DJ. He was screaming about suing me and hating me but my ears were muffled. Some great sadness swelled inside me and made the world seem small. I watched my left hand hold his shirt front and push him back against the wall. He hit me as I did this but the fog in my ears had spread into my body and I only observed the shudder in my sight rather than feeling the contact. I held him against the wall as he hit me again and again. I could hear or smell nothing. Fear was strobing through his eyes. I felt so dull. So muffled. Behind him was the reinforced window cracked in the shape of my head. I thought of that beautiful woman ravaged by his drugs. Her tongue lashing at her lips. The way she stretched her labia demanding something she didn't want. I thought of millions of ants crawling into my windpipe. He kept hitting me. I could see my blood on his hands, but still he was afraid. The ants were still crawling on me. I couldn't breathe, but it didn't concern me. The dullness was so familiar. It was so easy now to accept it. Time. I punched him with my right hand. His head was caught between the brick wall and my fist. His body jolted with the impact. He was still yelling or screaming and hitting at me. Ants. Dull. Hit. Hitting him felt good. Ants. The woman on the bed, and now she's screaming not moaning. I hit him again. And again. And again. My right arm was going like a piston. Back forth back forth back forth back forth. I noticed Oscar holding people back from stopping me. The DJ's blood ran thick over my left hand. It could have been hot or cold. My right hand kept going. His face was soft and splashing. My right hand was covered in his blood. He wasn't hitting me anymore. Ants. People were pulling me off. I let go. Ants. People were looking at the DJ, who was limp.

I liked it. It was so easy now to accept it.

Time.

Lou looked at me like I was a monster. It must be the ants, so many of them, still so hard to breathe.

I took the number twelve off my chest and dropped it.

I walked away from the club. People moved quickly out of the way as I moved up the lane. I walked home, my hands and face covered in blood and my body crawling with ants.

I called Johnny on Sunday and quit. He was relieved. It saved him firing me. I thought for a moment about my team-mates and how they would get on. But it was a fleeting concern. For the first time in six years I was not employed to be in danger.

I looked at myself in the mirror. My left cheek was puffy and cut in two places. My left eye was swollen and bloodshot. My shirt was new and looked good. I still looked fit and strong. The knuckles on my right hand were split. The scabs ached and sat on my hand like wet salami.

I picked Bec up from the gallery where she worked. I'd normally be just getting out of bed. She looked beautiful and clean. Most people I knew were sweaty or sleep-deprived at this time of day. She had on a denim skirt, tightly buttoned cotton shirt and the same slip-on shoes she'd worn the night I met her at the club. I'd picked up Vietnamese for lunch and we drove to a park.

'What happened to you?' she asked.

'Just some stuff at work.'

'Is that normal? That sort of … damage?'

'This is a little more than I'd expect from a normal weekend.'

'Oh. But fights are normal?'

'Fights are normal. But not big ones.'

'Big ones? Do you get hurt very often?'

'Sometimes. Why don't you tell me about what you do at the gallery?'

'Oh, not much. I do their online design. We don't generally get into fights.'

'Sounds great. Sun's nice.'

'Lovely. Don't you wish you worked somewhere safe?'

'I guess … nowhere is completely safe … safer would be good.'

The sun refracted in Bec's hair. Her skin had a smooth, sandy quality that was inviting. She was coy and proper. Reserved. I couldn't remember the last time I had been in the sun. I closed my eyes a moment against the brilliance of the sky's blue. The breath in my nostrils was clean and the heat of the day made me feel less hunted.

My Life in a Pea Soup
Lisa Nops
ISBN: 9781921462320

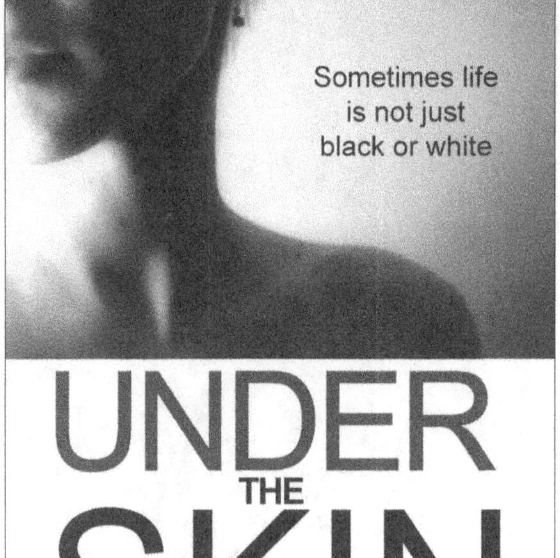

Under the Skin
Marion van Dyk
ISBN:9781921462801

False Start
Mark O'Flynn
ISBN:9781921462894

Catch Up With the Sun
Heidi Douglas
ISBN:9781921462368